The Catholic Working Mom's Guide to Life

"JoAnna Wahlund did more than live her life. She stepped back and analyzed her situation as Catholic Working mom, tackled the taboos, and now she provides the modern woman of faith a reasoned, can-do guide through all the major questions and dilemmas Catholic women in the workforce encounter. This book elegantly furthers the beauty of feminine genius more than any other in our time."

—**Stacy Trasancos,** wife, mother, nationally recognized author, speaker, and educator on the topic of theology and science

"As the creator and head fangirl at Catholic Working Mothers (FB), JoAnna Wahlund writes with pragmatism and empathy to those whose vocations include not just frying the bacon, but bringing it home as well. Regardless of why, where, or how much you work, this book will help you keep your priorities straight, your family close, and your soul connected to the God who sees it all ... and loves you more than you can imagine anyway."

— **Heidi Hess Saxton,** author and blogger, *Life on the Road Less Traveled*

"Whether you love your job or hate it, whether you are expecting your first baby or navigating child care for many kids, you will find a trusted companion in JoAnna's words—sage advice, helpful hints, and encouragement that you are never alone. Return to this book whenever you need to find peace in the multiple ways God has called you to share your love and spend your life, at home and at work!"

—**Laura Kelly Fanucci,** author of *Everyday Sacrament: The Messy Grace of Parenting* and *Grieving Together: A Couple's Journey through Miscarriage*

"*The Catholic Working Mom's Guide to Life* builds up Catholic womanhood by respectfully highlighting a large group of women who are often ignored or even shamed. JoAnna rallies all women to support one another in their vocations and shares relatable anecdotes to grow empathy and sisterhood. Wahlund is smart, strong, and incredibly approachable as a writer and shares helpful facts and insights so working moms can thrive in their careers and homes. I am convinced that all Catholic women should read this book so we can better support our sisters in Christ."

—**Bonnie L. Engstrom**, speaker, author, and blogger at *A Knotted Life*

"*The Catholic Working Mom's Guide to Life* is a gift for every mama who has wrestled with contributing to the family income while bringing up her children. It's practical and authentically Catholic guidance and advice — beginning and ending with the reminder to pray, pray, pray to discern God's will, and including the teachings of the Church and the examples set by saints who were working mothers — making it an essential resource for all women who have both babies and bosses."

—**Kate Morna Towne**, mother, freelance writer, blogger at
SanctaNomina.net, and author of *Catholic Baby Names for Girls and Boys:
Over 250 Ways to Honor Our Lady*

"*The Catholic Working Mom's Guide to Life* isn't just a memoir or a collection of theoretical essays on working moms; it's a field guide full of practical tips that can be implemented immediately. Workplace moms and stay-at-home-moms alike will benefit from the wisdom in these pages. Ultimately, this book is a pro-life work as it brings about understanding and highlights dignity across vocations."

—**Jenna Hines**, author and founder of *Call Her Happy*

"*The Catholic Working Mom's Guide to Life* is the first book of its kind. JoAnna has not only provided practical and concrete tools for working mothers everywhere, but she also speaks words of encouragement and inspiration that so many of us need to hear. This book is an excellent reminder that when God comes first, He gives us what we need to fulfill our mission both in our homes and in the workplace."

—**Deanna Johnston, MA**, Director of Family Life at the St. Philip Institute of Catechesis and Evangelization

"*The Catholic Working Mom's Guide to Life* by JoAnna Wahlund is a must-have resource for any mom employed outside the home. Combining both the spiritual and practical aspects of being a working mother facing the many challenges of a career, keeping a home, and raising holy and healthy children, she offers practical advice on finances, childcare, home management, prayer, fellowship, and many other choices working moms are faced with. Whether you are employed full-time, part-time, as a freelancer, or thinking about re-entering the work place after your children are older, this book offers straightforward tips and advice while keeping things real. This book is a welcome addition to any working woman's library."

—**Mary Lenaburg**, author of *Be Brave in the Scared*

"If you've ever felt alone or less-than as a working Catholic mother, *The Catholic Working Mom's Guide to Life* is a must-read. JoAnna's advice has been invaluable for me as I navigate this season of life myself."

—**Chloe Langr**, Catholic author, blogger, and creator of *Letters to Women* podcast

"I can always count on JoAnna Wahlund to get to the meat of the issue, cutting to the heart of the matter with chapter and verse of supporting arguments from the Catechism, Holy Scripture, and the lives of the saints. Wahlund is so good at pointing us back to the Church's love and shepherding in a logical, accessible, and heartfelt manner. I am honored to have my story included in its pages and I heartily recommend it to any woman — or man — who needs a guidance in discerning their vocation as a parent."

—**Amanda Martinez Beck**, author of *Lovely: How I Learned to Embrace the Body God Gave Me* and co-host of the *Fat & Faithful* podcast

The Catholic
Working Mom's
Guide to Life

JoAnna Wahlund

Our Sunday Visitor

www.osv.com
Our Sunday Visitor Publishing Division
Our Sunday Visitor, Inc.
Huntington, Indiana 46750

Except where noted, the Scripture citations used in this work are taken from the *Revised Standard Version of the Bible — Second Catholic Edition* (Ignatius Edition), copyright © 1965, 1966, 2006 National Council of the Churches of Christ in the United States of America.
Used by permission. All rights reserved.

Every reasonable effort has been made to determine copyright holders of excerpted materials and to secure permissions as needed. If any copyrighted materials have been inadvertently used in this work without proper credit being given in one form or another, please notify Our Sunday Visitor in writing so that future printings of this work may be corrected accordingly.

Copyright © 2019 by JoAnna Wahlund

24 23 22 21 20 19   1 2 3 4 5 6 7 8 9

All rights reserved. With the exception of short excerpts for critical reviews, no part of this work may be reproduced or transmitted in any form or by any means whatsoever without permission from the publisher. For more information, visit: www.osv.com/permissions.

Our Sunday Visitor Publishing Division
Our Sunday Visitor, Inc.
200 Noll Plaza
Huntington, IN 46750
1-800-348-2440

ISBN: 978-1-68192-325-3 (Inventory No. T1997)
eISBN: 978-1-68192-326-0
LCCN: 2019936312

Cover and interior design: Chelsea Alt
Cover and interior art: Shutterstock

Printed in the United States of America

This book is dedicated to my husband, Collin, who believed in my dream and supported me in all my efforts to make it happen; my children, Elanor, William, Violet, Gabriel, Peter, and Laura, who are my most precious gifts from God; and Catholic working mothers everywhere.

Contents

Contents

Chapter 1

You Are Not Alone

Most of the books and blogs written for and about Catholic mothers take for granted that the bulk of their time is devoted to their household and children. These publications support and encourage women in their vocations as wives and mothers, but seem to assume that these are women's only vocations.

However, many Catholic mothers have felt called by God to work outside the home, serving others with their talents. Many Catholic mothers have determined that they must work, even if they'd prefer to stay home, in order to provide for their families.

While all mothers work hard on a daily basis, mothers who earn a wage in addition to the responsibilities of their roles as wives and parents often face a unique set of challenges. With multiple vocations, it's all they can do to keep up with the bare minimum of housework, cooking, and laundry in addition to working twenty, thirty, forty, or more hours per week (plus the time it might take for commuting and daycare drop-off/pickup).

I am intimately familiar with the joys and challenges of this hectic lifestyle, because I lived it for more than a decade.

My journey as a Catholic working mother began on May 17, 2004. As I watched the pregnancy test turn positive, my heart rejoiced, but my brain said, "How are you going to afford a child?"

That was a question my husband and I returned to again and again over the next several months. I was working full time, and he was working part time while going to college. I was a fairly new college graduate working in an entry-level job, and my income alone would not cover all of our expenses. We determined that, after the baby was born, we could work opposite shifts for the first six months to avoid paying for daycare; after that, we would reassess.

As the child of a working mother, I assumed that returning to work after my six weeks of unpaid leave — which was all we could (barely) afford — would be a matter of course. But after my first child and eldest daughter was born on January 13, 2005, I found that, unexpectedly, my heart longed to stay home with her. I had underestimated how incredibly difficult and heart-wrenching it would be to leave her in another's care—even my husband's — while I went to work.

We revisited our financial situation time and time again, especially after my husband made the decision to postpone his education and start working full time, but our calculations always

> "Even though I would actually love to be at home more but can't, I love [the Catholic Working Mothers Facebook] group because it is filled with faithful, strong Catholic women who are living their faith out in the real world. This doesn't make us any less of wonderful mothers than our SAHM friends, and it allows us to be a witness to our coworkers, customers, and others we wouldn't otherwise interact with were it not for working outside the home."
> — Erin G.

ended the same: we needed two incomes, even after the cost of daycare.

As my child grew and I tried to make friends with other Catholic mothers in my area, as well as online, I slowly began to realize that I seemed to be unique in Catholic circles.

Most Catholic mothers with young children in my parish and in online groups were stay-at-home-mothers (SAHMs), but I was a Catholic mother with a young child who worked outside the home.

I found it difficult to relate to the Catholic SAHMs who didn't have to figure out how to juggle meal planning, cooking, laundry, and cleaning while absent from the home forty hours per week. No one could empathize with my struggle to balance spending time with my daughter and husband on weekends while struggling to complete all the household tasks that had piled up during the week.

The other mothers I met had never had to play "The Sick Time Shuffle" with their husband, trying to figure out who had the most paid time off left and whose boss would be more sympathetic to the need to call in sick when the baby was ill and couldn't go to daycare. They've never had to figure out what to do when the room in which you pump breast milk at work is constantly in use by others.

There were non-Catholic moms with young children who worked outside the home; but again, there was a divide. They didn't understand the challenges I faced while using natural family planning to avoid pregnancy. Often, my Catholic views on hot-button issues such as abortion or same-sex marriage (I've been asked to leave more than one secular online mom's group due to perceived bigotry) or even something as simple as finding a Mass time outside of working hours on holy days of obligation would sound the death knell for a friendship.

I did make some friends, both Catholic and non-Catholic, but

I often wished for a circle of women who could understand the struggles I faced as I juggled my multiple roles of wife, mother, and employee. For a long while, I felt utterly alone. We moved across the country a few years later, and by then our family had expanded from one child to five.

I balanced (often awkwardly) my faith, my work, and my family life. I struggled with feelings of isolation and loneliness as I read with envy the "mommy blogs" of Catholic women who stayed at home with their children and electronically eavesdropped on their lives in various Facebook groups for Catholic mothers — groups in which I always felt like something of an outsider.

One morning, I received a Facebook message from Jenny, a friend of a friend, who introduced herself as a fellow Catholic working mother with small children. Our mutual friend had suggested that she contact me since we were in similar circumstances — both of us reluctantly working full time, because our families needed the income.

Jenny remarked in her message, "I hope we can be a source of community when nobody around us understands what it is like to live like we do."

She's absolutely right, I thought. We really needed a source of community, given that it seemed as if no one around us understood what it was like to constantly try to balance faith, work, and family in a culture that was increasingly hostile to Catholicism. I wondered, not for the first time, why no one had created a Facebook group specifically for Catholic working mothers.

At that moment, I could almost feel the Holy Spirit figuratively smacking me upside the head. *Why haven't you started one?* I could almost hear him asking me.

I think my hesitation was a result of viewing my status as a Catholic working mother as temporary, just until my husband was earning enough to allow me to stay at home. But here we were, almost fourteen years and five kids later, and I was still working. My husband had been laid off from his job several months before and hadn't yet found another — making me the primary breadwinner, at least for the time being. He had finally earned his degree, and the prospect of him quickly finding a job with an income large enough to cover all our expenses as a new college grad was very slim.

It was time, I decided, to embrace my life and my status as a Catholic working mother, instead of treating it as a temporary condition that would someday end.

On August 8, 2014, with a few clicks on my smartphone, the Catholic Working Mothers Facebook group was born. Less than a year later, it had more than four hundred members. As of this writing in 2019, we've grown to more than five thousand. I've gone from being the sole administrator to managing a volunteer staff of seven additional moderators who help keep the group running smoothly.

It's truly an amazing community of women that has spawned some very close-knit ties and friendships. As C. S. Lewis says in *The Four Loves*: "Friendship, I have said, is born at the moment

> *"I've been feeling guilty about being away from my kids so much, and I was talking to my therapist about it. We came up with the idea of not a single ideal, but an infinite amount of families with an infinite amount of right ways to run their families ... everybody doing what's right for their own families. I'm a Trekkie so it made me think of the Vulcan 'infinite diversity in infinite combinations.' So now every time I feel guilty, I just think of Spock applauding all these working mamas' infinite combinations!"*
>
> *— Rosie H.*

when one man says to another 'What! You too? I thought that no one but myself.'"

It has become a source of encouragement and inspiration for those of us who are struggling to balance the duties of their vocations as mothers with the responsibilities of being wage earners, whether outside of the home or from the home.

Without a doubt, the most common refrain I hear from fellow Catholic working mothers when they happen upon me or the Facebook group is something along the lines of, "I thought I was the only one!" One woman, upon finding out about the group, quipped, "I can't believe there are more people like me. I felt like a Catholic unicorn."

According to the Pew Research Center, 40 percent of working mothers in the United States are the sole or primary wage earners for their families.[1] It's getting harder and harder to support a family — especially a large family — on one income alone.

There are Catholic families for whom the mother is the primary breadwinner because the father stays at home with the children, or is disabled, or absent due to divorce or abandonment, or deceased.

More frequently, though, rising food and housing costs, medical insurance needs, and crippling student loan and medical debt all contribute to a situation where both a mother and a father need to earn income to support their family.

If you're Catholic, there's a good chance that your family may be a large one by society's standards, which already sets us apart. If a Catholic working mother is a unicorn in today's world, even more so is the Catholic mother who works *and* has four or more young children. I regularly saw dropped jaws and bugged-out eyes when people found out that I had six children and worked full time outside the home.

This situation can feel extremely isolating, and very, very lonely. Added to that is the difficulty of finding and making other Catholic mom friends when you work forty hours per week (or sometimes more) and need to spend evenings and weekends doing housework, laundry, grocery shopping, etc.

However, if you are a Catholic working mother of any variety, know this: you are not alone!

We are members of a very diverse Church, and as such we are a diverse people. We are of different races and ethnicities; we're located in the United States and in other countries around the world; we inhabit

> "Some of us choose to work because we love our careers. Some of us have to out of necessity. Regardless of why we work, we do our best each and every day to ensure that our kids are holy, healthy, and loved!"
> — Angela M.

different economic and educational tiers. While we come from unique backgrounds and have differing perspectives, there are three common threads that tie us together:

We are Catholic. We are lay Catholic women—cradle Catholics, converts, or reverts — who are faithful to the magisterium of the Catholic Church. We hold, believe, and practice all that the one, holy, Catholic, and apostolic Church teaches, believes, and proclaims to be true, whether from the natural moral law or by way of revelation from God through Scripture and Tradition. We strive to live out our faith in word and in deed in every aspect of our lives.

We are working. We earn a wage in addition to our responsibilities as mothers. Some of us work part time; some of us work full time. Some of us are freelancers or in-home daycare providers; some of us are executives, teachers, nurses, or retail employees. Some of us have spouses who work, and some of us are the primary breadwinners for our families while our spouse is in school or stays at home. Some of us are single, separated, divorced, or widowed. Some of us are working by choice, called by God to fulfill a specific vocation; some of us work because our income is necessary to support our families and meet our financial obligations.

We are mothers. Some of us are pregnant. Some of us have children by adoption. Some of us have one or two children. Some of us have three or more children. Some of us have children in heaven. Some of us have stepchildren. All of us recognize that our vocation as a mother is one of the most important jobs we will ever have.

We don't compete with stay-at-home moms (SAHMs) — we complement them. We both have tremendously important responsibilities with equally difficult concerns and unique challenges. Some of us may transition over time depending on our season of life, whether that means going from a SAHM to working outside the home, or becoming a SAHM after many years of outside employment.

Much like the communion of saints, there is a whole community of Catholic working mothers out there who are walking a similar path, and it is out of their collective wisdom and sharing of experiences that this book was born.

I'll talk more in depth about finding your community in chapter 11. But for now, let me reiterate: You are not alone.

Chapter 2

Our Sisters, the Saints

I 'm the daughter of a working mother. My mother was, and still is, a teacher, and many times during my childhood she was the sole breadwinner for our family. Most of my female relatives work outside the home, and many of my elementary school teachers were working mothers.

I wasn't raised Catholic, and working mothers were not unusual in the Protestant denomination I grew up in. As a child, I knew that some of my classmates had mothers who didn't work outside the home, but my experience was such that I viewed SAHMs as the exception, not the norm.

Imagine my confusion, as a fairly new Catholic convert and new working mother, when I first encountered fellow Catholics who firmly believed that the teaching of the Catholic Church was that mothers shouldn't work outside the home as a general rule. They believed that there may be extreme cases in which a mother who was widowed (or worse, divorced or unmarried) might need to work, but that those cases needed to be few and far between, and that the woman needed to find herself a Catholic husband as soon as possible so she could quit her job and raise her children.

Is this an accurate reflection of what the Church taught or

teaches about working mothers?

Well, sort of ... but not really.

The Church *does* teach that a father is obligated to support his family ... but it *doesn't* teach that *only* the father may or should support the family.

The Church *does* teach that a father should not force or pressure his wife to work outside the home, or expect that she will without discussing it with her ... but it *doesn't* teach that a wife must never work outside the home except in "extraordinary" circumstances, or must never desire to work outside the home.

The Church *does* teach that a mother should keep up a good home and raise her children properly ... but it *doesn't* teach that a mother can only do this if she doesn't work outside the home.

The Church *does* teach that greed or selfishness should not cause parents to neglect their children ... but it *doesn't* teach that a mother who works does so due to motives of greed or selfishness.

The *Catechism of the Catholic Church* and papal encyclicals throughout history are great resources on the subject of working mothers. However, what I find most compelling in regard to this discussion is the lives of the saints, whom we are encouraged to emulate in our own lives.

Several biblical figures and saints were working mothers. They may not have been "working" in the sense that we know it today, where a mother typically leaves the house in the morning, works in an external location, and returns home every evening, but they worked nonetheless.

For instance, the woman described in Proverbs 31 had several occupations — even reading that chapter makes me tired! She "seeks wool and flax, and works with willing hands" (31:13). She "considers a field and buys it; with the fruit of her hands she plants a vineyard" (31:14). She "puts her hands to the distaff, and her hands hold the spindle" (31:19). She "opens her hand to the poor, and reaches out her hands to the needy" (31:20). She "makes linen garments and sells them; she delivers girdles to the merchant" (31:24). All that, and she looks to the needs of her household, including managing a staff of servants!

Priscilla and Lydia, two women mentioned in the New Testament, also may have been working mothers, although this is not explicitly stated. Priscilla was married to Aquila, and they worked together as tent-makers. Later, they traveled with the Apostle Paul. We don't know if they had children, but I have found at least one icon that features Priscilla and Aquila as parents.[2]

Lydia was a seller of purple cloth. It is speculated that Lydia was a widow, indicated by the fact that she was able to invite strangers — and strange men, at that — to reside in her home, a freedom unheard of for a single or currently married woman at that time. The Bible mentions that she had her "entire household" baptized — a household that may have included her own children (cf. Acts 16:14–15).

> "My job doesn't interfere with my vocation, it wonderfully ties into and supports it. In the same way, my husband's job supports his vocation of fatherhood. He makes sure it doesn't get in the way by keeping strict working hours and setting limits with his bosses so they know that he won't sell his soul and all of his waking hours to the office. His vocation of fatherhood is equally important to mine of motherhood. Yes, they look different, but this isn't a concern that only occurs with working mothers. It just isn't."
>
> — *Amy G.*

The communion of canonized saints also counts several working mothers among its number. One whom I only recently learned

> "We cannot 'cookie-cutter'
> every mom into 24/7
> SAHMs, if working is what
> helps their husband — (and
> their entire family) — to pay
> the bills/save/whatever. It
> is a very hard struggle for
> some in ministry, clerical,
> or lay. And so we gently
> witness that God made
> us all differently, and
> our families to function
> differently, than some
> 'ideal.'"
> — Naomi B.

about is Saint Frances of Rome. An excellent patroness for the reluctant working woman, her dearest desire was to devote herself to religious life. However, her father commanded her to marry instead, and after a long interior struggle, she submitted her life to God's will. She and her husband had several children, and in addition to managing her household, she devoted herself to charitable work — including running a hospital for the poor.

Saint Elizabeth Ann Seton converted to Catholicism after being widowed. Although she was the sole caretaker for her five children, she founded a school and a religious order. The order "made provisions for Elizabeth to continue raising her children" while she worked as a teacher.[3]

One of my favorite saints is Saint Zélie Martin, mother of Saint Thérèse of Lisieux. In addition to being a faithful Catholic wife and mother, she was also a working professional. Before her marriage, she learned the craft of lace-making, and she was so talented in her field that she started her own business. Her clientele and reputation grew to the point that her husband, who had been a watchmaker, elected to leave his own business in order to join his wife's!

Saint Zélie was an amazing example of a working mother. Per the Carmelite Sisters in Ireland:

That same year [1870] Louis sold his business to his

nephew so that he could help Zélie with hers. He had already taken over the bookkeeping and was now free to travel to obtain orders. Zélie had fifteen women working for her in their own homes, and every Thursday they brought her the work they had done and received the cotton and their instructions for the next week. Zélie assembled the pieces that they brought to her. She often worked late into the night as she always gave time to her children when they needed it and she wrote many letters especially to her two eldest daughters when they were in boarding school.[4]

Note that Zélie not only placed her elder daughters in boarding school, but she also gave over the care of her youngest daughter to a nurse for the first eighteen months of her life, per the Society of the Little Flower:

> Due to Thérèse's weak and frail condition at birth, she was taken care of by a nurse for her first year and a half. Because of this care, she became a lively, mischievous, and self-confident child.[5]

Given that all five of Zélie's surviving daughters eventually entered religious life — and several of them are either saints or on the path to sainthood — it doesn't seem like they were much harmed by having a working mother or going to "daycare"!

Another inspirational saint for working mothers is Saint Edith Stein, also known as Saint Teresa Benedicta of the Cross, a Jewish convert to the faith and brilliant philosopher who was killed in a Nazi concentration camp.

Although Stein had a vocation to religious life instead of one to marriage and family, and thus only experienced spiritual motherhood, she was a gifted academic and philosopher who penned a large volume of work and gave many lectures regarding the nature and vocation of women.

In her *Essays on Woman*, she notes in a 1931 lecture titled "The Separate Vocations of Men and Women According to Nature and Grace," that "the question whether women should enter the professional life or stay at home has been controversial for some time."

Later in this particular essay, she discusses the economic situation that has made women in the workforce a reality and asks, "On the whole[,] does woman's professional life outside of the home violate the order of nature and grace? I believe that one must answer 'no' to this question."

She continues:

> Wherever the circle of domestic duties is too narrow for the wife to attain the full formation of her powers, both nature and reason concur that she reach out beyond this circle. It appears to me, however, that there is a limit to such professional activities whenever it jeopardizes domestic life, i.e., the community of life and formation consisting of parents and children. It seems to me a contradiction of the divine order when the professional activities of the husband escalate to a degree which cuts him off completely from family life. This is even more true of the wife. Any social condition is an unhealthy one which compels married women to seek gainful employment and makes it impossible for them to manage their home. And we should accept as normal that the married woman is restricted to domestic life at a time when her household duties exact her total energies.[6]

Here Edith Stein reiterates the teachings of the popes: It is not inherently wrong or sinful for a mother to work outside the home, but such work should not cause the neglect of home and family — and that goes for the husband as well. She decries social conditions that *compel* women to seek gainful employment — the implication being that they do so against their will, due to economic conditions — AND (not "or") make it impossible for them to manage their home.

Additionally, the last line of this quote makes the case for extended maternity leave long before such policies were even proposed, let alone enacted.

I would love to reprint her essay (not to mention several others) in its entirety, but it would make this chapter entirely too long. I highly recommend reading her works, especially the essays in this particular volume, as they are brilliant discourses on theological issues that are pertinent to Catholic women, whether they are single, married, or in religious life.

Of course, no book about working mothers would be complete without discussion of our patroness: Saint Gianna Beretta Molla.

Saint Gianna was born in 1922 in Milan, Italy, into a devout Catholic family. Her solid faith and dedication to prayer led her to devote her life to the service of others. She realized this vocation by studying medicine, becoming a doctor, and opening her own pediatrics practice, while also serving the poor and elderly through volunteer work. She discerned a vocation to marriage and family, and was wedded to Pietro Molla, an engineer, on September 24, 1955. Following her marriage, she had three children in four years while continuing to work as a pediatrician.

In the first trimester of her fourth pregnancy, Gianna was diagnosed with a dangerously large fibroid tumor in her uterus. Per Catholic teaching, a therapeutic hysterectomy was a morally licit option under the principle of double effect, but Gianna chose a riskier surgery to remove only the fibroid in an attempt to save the baby.

The surgery was successful, but the remainder of her pregnancy was fraught with anxiety as it was unknown what effects or complications the surgery might have had on the baby, and the

> *"[H]opefully, in addition to the working moms already canonized, WE can be the people our Catholic friends hold up as examples of someone who is a good Catholic and working mom, doing good work, and being a good mom."*
>
> *— Katie F.*

early surgery also made her subsequent delivery riskier as well. Throughout, Gianna insisted that, if a choice had to be made, she wanted her husband and medical providers to save the baby, not her.

Her fourth child, a girl christened Gianna Emanuela, was eventually born safely, but the delivery included complications that claimed Saint Gianna's life one week later. She died on April 28, 1962. On April 24, 1994, she was beatified by Saint John Paul II, and canonized by him on May 16, 2004. Her husband and children were present at her canonization.

Gianna did not undertake work outside the home due to financial necessity; her husband was an engineer, and his income would have been more than adequate for his family's needs. Instead, she worked outside the home because she felt she had been called by God to serve the members of her community as a doctor, while also serving her husband and children as a wife and mother. Per her biography on the Vatican website, "with simplicity and equilibrium she harmonized the demands of mother, wife, doctor, and her passion for life."[7]

It is true that Gianna had made the decision to give up her medical practice once her fourth child was born, but her decision was not because she had come to the conclusion that working outside the home was somehow wrong or inappropriate. As her husband, Pietro, said in a biography about his wife:

Already during our engagement, Gianna had asked me about continuing her profession at least as long as her obligations as wife and above all as mother allowed it. I did not oppose that because I knew well how enthusiastically she practiced medicine, how attached she was to her patients. Later, by mutual agreement, we made the decision that she would stop at the birth of our fourth child. In this understanding, she continued her profession until her last confinement.[8]

A study of Saint Gianna's life, including the letters she wrote to her husband, reveals a devout woman who had been immersed in the teachings of the Catholic Church from childhood, and who was devoted to serving God in all aspects of her life. She lived a life of heroic virtue, as is evidenced by the fact that she was canonized as a saint.

May we all be so skilled as Saint Gianna in managing our varied vocations as wives, mothers, and working women!

Chapter 3
Finding Peace When You Don't Want to Work

When my husband and I married, he did not have a college degree, and he was working as an independent contractor for an IT staffing firm. I had just started my junior year of college and was working part time. Our plan was for both of us to obtain our degrees before we started a family. Then, we figured, we'd have three or *maybe* four kids. Once we were done having kids, one of us would get sterilized.

Our carefully laid plans were completely upended by our conversion to Catholicism two years later. For the first time, we learned about the Church's teaching regarding the gift of children, responsible parenthood, and discernment of family size. We also were introduced to Natural Family Planning. According to the United States Conference of Catholic Bishops, NFP "represents the only authentic approach to family planning available to husbands and wives because these methods can be used to both attempt or avoid pregnancy."[9] To our surprise, we felt a call to become parents much sooner than we'd originally planned — after I had earned my degree, but before my husband had earned his.

Because I had a college degree, I had more earning power than my husband. I became a working mother; and as events transpired, I was a reluctant working mother for approximately thirteen years. I wasn't working because I felt a calling to be in that particular field, or in that particular profession, or at that particular company. I worked only because we needed my income to help pay our bills.

Yes, daycare was a significant cost; in fact, our daycare bill was more than our rent, and then more than our mortgage, once we bought a house. Yet I still made enough money after daycare expenses and taxes to pay bills. I was sometimes the sole provider of health insurance for our family as well.

I've had many conversations with other Catholic working mothers who are in the same boat. It is getting harder and harder these days to scrape by on one income alone. Inflation has skyrocketed, along with the cost of living, but salaries haven't kept pace.

Job security is a thing of the past — it's increasingly rare to hear of someone who has stayed at the same company more than ten years, let alone someone who started out in an entry-level role and worked up to a senior role.

Another factor is that so many of us have graduated from college with crushing student-loan debt. When I was in high school, the prevailing attitude seemed to be that you *needed* a college degree to get a decent job, and that student loans were a necessary evil. As such, I went to college and acquired a massive load of student-loan debt — debt that I am still paying off.

It used to be that you could work part time while going to college, or perhaps work full time during the summers, and use the money you earned to pay your tuition as well as your living expenses and textbooks, but that simply isn't feasible anymore.

College tuition isn't the only expense that has skyrocketed in the past few decades. Groceries, housing, utilities, and gasoline have all gone up, and wages haven't kept pace with inflation. When you consider the cost of groceries, utilities, and healthcare — all necessities — it proves difficult to pay even the basic expenses without two incomes.

Thus, many Catholic mothers need to work, either part time or full time, to help support their families. There are families for whom the mother is the primary breadwinner because she has the higher earning potential; in some cases, the father stays at home with the children or only works part time.

Some Catholic mothers work so that their family can afford Catholic school tuition for their children, as that expense

"I don't get over [the guilt] altogether, but what helps me is a) taking a look at our budget and knowing that we realistically could not make it work for me to stay home right now and b) recognizing that God reveals his will through circumstances, even if I don't like them. Since our circumstances are pretty clearly indicating that I need to work right now, I recognize that my feelings of guilt are unwarranted, and use them to pray for trust and detachment — we are stewards of our children, but they ultimately belong to God. Whenever I have rough drop-off days, it helps me to remember to say a prayer to their guardian angels and the Blessed Mother to keep them safe and happy."
— *Lisa W.*

has also skyrocketed in the past few decades. Could a family make it on one income if they put their kids in public school or homeschooled instead of sending their kids to Catholic school? Maybe, but for those parents, a Catholic education is a priority, and not all parents are cut out to homeschool.

Then there are the Catholic mothers who need to work due to difficult family circumstances: They are single, separated, divorced, or widowed, and they are the only means of support for their children.

Whatever your situation, you can find comfort in the fact that you are doing what is necessary to support your family. However, knowing this intellectually doesn't stop a working mother from being emotionally plagued by guilt.

Guilt: The Working Mother's Constant Companion

The reasons a family might need a second income are many and varied, but that doesn't prevent others from thinking they know better than you do when it comes to your family's circumstances.

While the Church does not teach that mothers cannot work, that doesn't keep others from sharing their opinions on the subject. It's difficult to battle the perception by certain fellow Catholics that you don't *need* to work; in fact, it's remarkably similar to battling the perception by non-Catholics that you have too many children (or the perception by some Catholics that you have too few children).

I once had someone message me on Facebook and say that she could tell from my blog that I didn't need to work full time, since I'd hired a professional photographer to take pictures of my kids — obviously, if I could afford to do that, I could afford to stay at home if I just gave up such luxuries.

The reality was that the photo shoot was a mini session that cost $50, one that I paid for with birthday money I'd received earlier in the month. The shoot also paid for itself because I turned those pictures into inexpensive Christmas gifts for grandparents by creating photo books online using discount coupons.

Despite the fact that I knew this person's criticisms were unreasonable and unwarranted, I still felt a twinge of guilt.

Guilt, unfortunately, is often the reluctant working mother's constant companion. Guilt when you drop off the kids at daycare and they don't want to go. Guilt if they happen to hit a milestone while at daycare and you don't see it. Guilt when evenings are filled with errands or extracurriculars or even just dinner preparations and cleanup instead of quality time with your kids. Guilt when you're eager for the kids' bedtime because all you want to do is turn your brain off and watch a show on Netflix with your husband.

Guilt when a child wants you to chaperone a field trip, or has an in-class party or awards ceremony, but you're completely out of paid time off. Or worse, guilt when your children are sick, and even though it's breaking your heart to leave them with their father or a sympathetic relative or neighbor, you can't afford to take an unpaid day or there's a meeting you *can't* miss, short of a dire emergency.

I can also attest to the fact that stay-at-home mothers aren't immune to mom guilt. After being laid off twice in the span of one year, I decided to take a break from the workforce for a while (primarily so I could concentrate on writing this book). I was still wracked with guilt — guilt that I wasn't getting enough housework done, guilt that I was spending more time doing housework and writing than with my kids, guilt that I wasn't contributing financially to the household like I had before. It never ends.

As actress Anna Faris puts it, "Motherhood is like a big sleeping bag of guilt."[10]

It may not be possible to get rid of the guilt entirely, but you can turn it into a tool for good. Use that guilt as encouragement to prioritize your tasks and stay focused on your children so that you can be completely present for them during the times when you *are* home. Focus on providing your children with quality time in lieu of a quantity of time.

Remember that guilt is often Satan's way of trying to infuse us with depression and self-doubt. He loves to hit us where it hurts and whisper in our ear, "If you were a better mother, you wouldn't be working right now; you'd be with your child."

Sometimes, we have to be firm and say, "Get thee behind me, Satan!" whenever those niggling feelings of guilt start creeping into our heads. God gives us conviction and the strength to make the changes we need to make — he does not give us condemnation.

Also remember this: If it was God's plan for you to be home, you would be. Like the Blessed Virgin Mary, you are being faithful by saying "yes" to God's will, even if his plan was not one you had envisioned for your life.

God may have you in your current situation for a reason. Maybe in the capacity of your employment, you will affect the lives of a client or a coworker or a customer for the better, bringing them closer to God. Or maybe God is protecting you from a financial pitfall that would otherwise transpire. But whatever the reason, as long as you have carefully and intentionally discerned the will of God for your life, you can be confident in knowing that you are where he needs you to be, even if you can't immediately see your place in his larger plan.

For example, I often prayed for our circumstances to change so that I could be a stay-at-home-mom, but it took thirteen years for that prayer to be answered. In hindsight, I can see that God's plan for me was to form the Catholic Working Mothers Facebook support group, which has now touched the lives of thousands of women. If God had answered that prayer on my timeline instead of his, the group might never have been created, and those women would not have gotten the support that they needed at that time in their lives.

Another tactic that helps with the guilt is to reframe the aspect of the situation that is making you feel guilty and look at it from a different perspective. For example, a CWM in my group was lamenting about how hurt she felt that her toddler, when asked where his mommy was by a friend, said, "At a meeting, working, working, working."

I asked her, "If he had that same reply when asked where his father was, would that be equally as hurtful?"

She said, "That's a really good question … and helpful to consider. I don't think AS hurtful, very true."

It's a fact that kids with working parents are missing out on time with them — but that is true whether the parent is the mother *or* the father. I'm pretty sure that same child would also miss things like healthcare, good food, reliable shelter, and other necessities that his mother's income helps to provide if she did not work.

The Daycare Dilemma

By and large, the biggest source of guilt for reluctant working mothers is putting our children in the care of others while we work. It seems to be somewhat more acceptable if we have husbands who are SAHDs, or if we have relatives who care for our children; but if we put our children in daycare, we are "paying someone else to raise our kids" or "letting our kids be raised by strangers."

Unless you take your kid to a new daycare every day, or you take your child to a center where turnover is unusually high (as in, new employees are hired and fired on a daily or weekly basis), strangers aren't raising your child. Instead, your child is forming close bonds with an adult who cares about him or her.

Furthermore, even stay-at-home parents aren't engaging their children one hundred percent of the time. A stay-at-home-parent does housework, reads, visits with friends, shops for groceries, brings the kids to playdates where they play with other kids, perhaps does volunteer work, blogs, spends time on social media, etc. What's the metric for gauging how much one-on-one time constitutes raising versus not raising? Is there a mathematical formula?

> *"Honestly, I put staying home out of my head. For me it was an impossible pipe dream that would have required winning the lottery because my husband is disabled; but still it was something I had always wanted, and I was disappointed. Happiness is more about perception than reality. If your heart is somewhere other than your reality, you're going to be unhappy. If you can't change your reality, change your heart."*
>
> — *Carrie K.*

If we want to foster a culture of life in this country, we *must* stop denigrating daycare. Most single moms need to work to support their kids, and a lot of mothers who choose life and keep their children instead of giving them up for adoption must, by necessity, place their child in daycare.

If it is the quantity of time that parents spend with their children that equates to "raising" them, then logically *only mothers* raise their children. Fathers do not, since (presumably) the father is working forty or more hours per week and only sees his children evenings, weekends, and holidays. Yet Catholics speak about both parents raising their children, as does the Church. How can this be, if the mother is the only one doing the raising?

What those with this mindset do not realize is that a good daycare *complements* our parenting; it does not replace it, much as schools do not replace parents as the primary educators of their children, but instead serve as a supplement to a child's education. Those who criticize daycare seem to be under the impression that all daycares are designed to expose young children to secular modernism and hedonism.

While centers like the ones they envision may exist, they certainly aren't like any of the ones I've had experience with, or have sent my children to in the past. They've obviously never seen my kids' former daycare, which was a home daycare run by a Mormon husband-and-wife team with four kids of their own. I know from experience that they shared many of the same moral values that I do as a Catholic, and they were also very respectful of our Catholic Faith (just as I was respectful of their Mormon faith).

Their house was clean and neat (much cleaner than my house, for sure!). They had a huge playroom with lots of toys, and a big backyard with artificial turf and play equipment, plus a misting system for hot months. They took field trips, played games, and read stories with the kids. They provided two nutritious meals a day plus a snack in the afternoon. My kids were in their care from 2011 to 2017, and they've cared for all six of my children — three of them since they were eight weeks old, and one since she was a year old. They became good friends, and I felt blessed and reassured that my children were in excellent hands while I worked to help support our family.

Similarly, the daycare we used from 2017 to 2018 was an in-home daycare run by a wonderful Christian woman who loved our kids as if they were her own. My kids loved her in return, and we remain friends to this day.

The stories from other Catholic working mothers are similar. We aren't tossing our kids into gulags while we traipse off to work every day. We put a lot of time and effort into finding a daycare situation that is a good fit for our family and complements our parenting. Some CWMs choose to employ nannies or au pairs. Some have relatives watch over their children. Some CWMs don't use daycare at all, and work opposite shifts or have their spouse stay at home with the children, or even work as daycare providers.

Whatever situation we choose, we make sure that our children are happy and well-cared for — and if we have concerns, we resolve them or find alternate arrangements. We can plainly see that our kids are happy, healthy, and thriving in the care of people we know and trust.

Resentment Is the Greatest Enemy of Contentment

Guilt isn't always bad, though. Our culture likes to joke about "Catholic guilt," but guilt can be a positive thing when it is the result of a certain situation or action clashing with our well-formed conscience. It's a good idea to analyze any situation or incident that is making you feel guilty and explore what changes you could have made or can make in the future. Sometimes there are no changes you can make, and you're doing exactly what you need to do. But there might be a step you can take or an action you can perform that will bring you closer to what your ideal is, and alleviate some of that guilt.

If you are desperately longing to be a SAHM, to the point where it's causing anger and resentment in your life, talk to your husband. Go over your finances together — your income, your expenses, your debt-to-income ratio, your short- and long-term financial goals. Discuss what needs to be done to make your dream a reality. Sometimes just having a plan and a goal to work toward can help ease the guilt. Even having a clearer picture of what circumstances would need to change in order for you to stop working can make you feel more confident in knowing that you're doing the right thing in your current situation.

Sometimes, however, the above approach isn't feasible (for example, if you're a single mother). I saw a quote on Twitter last year that said, "Resentment is the greatest enemy of contentment." If you are actively resenting your job, your boss, your coworkers, your general situation, or other aspects of your life, you're going to be much more susceptible to guilt, and it's going to be a lot harder to enjoy what you have if you're constantly obsessing about what you don't have or want to have.

I remember one day that was really rough for me. I was tired of commuting three hours round trip every day, tired of working, tired of constantly feeling like I couldn't keep up with the laundry, the dishes, the cooking. I found some satisfaction in my work, and I knew that my salary was necessary for my family's financial survival, but trying to balance a full-time job with full-time motherhood of (at that time) four young children seemed more difficult by the day.

I spent an hour of my commute sobbing as I cried out to God, telling him that I felt like I was Sisyphus — forever pushing my boulder up the hill, alone, unsupported, with no relief in sight. I arrived at work emotionally exhausted but feeling slightly better for having poured out my troubles.

> *"The concept of ONE or TWO people (the mother and father usually) being the sole nurturer, provider, caretaker, driver, supporter, etc. of their child is a completely new concept. For years we had generational caretakers. Multiple generations in the home would take care of the whole family. It was a group effort. In places like India and Japan, this is still a very common practice. In America, we have the means and the social expectation to live in our own separate homes, and that means separating our lives as well. Do not feel guilty that it takes a village. For years we had villages. People just very quickly forget that."*
> — *Hannah D.*

Throughout the day, I received encouraging e-mail messages from friends — even though I hadn't shared my struggle with any of them. Another friend wrote a blog post about Saint Francis de Sales that included this quote, which was immensely comforting:

Do not look forward in fear to the changes in life; rather,

look to them with full hope that as they arise, God, whose very own you are, will lead you safely through all things; and when you cannot stand it, God will carry you in his arms. Do not fear what may happen tomorrow; the same understanding Father who cares for you today will take care of you then and every day. He will either shield you from suffering or will give you unfailing strength to bear it. Be at peace, and put aside all anxious thoughts and imaginations.

I found that quote so helpful that I printed it out and hung it in my cubicle. It helped me realize that I wasn't Sisyphus, pushing my immense burden uphill all by myself, unless I *chose* to be Sisyphus. I had a burden, that's true, but that didn't make me any different from any other human being on this earth. Instead of struggling alone with a burden that was insurmountable, I could choose to be like Jesus, carrying my cross of reluctantly working with patience and offering up my sufferings for others.

As long as I viewed my trials and sufferings as burdens I had to deal with by myself, I would be a victim; but instead, I could learn to view my suffering as a work of love for others and be more like Jesus.

"Offering it up" is a concept that is foreign to many, even those raised in the Catholic Church. The more I thought about it, though, the more it made sense. It was not God's will for the world to contain suffering, but it was one of the consequences of the free will of our first parents. Adam and Eve chose to sin, and God respected their choice — even though it meant his beloved sons and daughters would have to suffer.

God, however, has given us the ability to take our suffering and use it for the good of others. As he so often does, he will bring good out of a bad situation. Our suffering does not have to be in vain, whether it is suffering caused from physical pain, emotional damage, or just the common trials of everyday life — including working when we would much rather be at home with our children.

While investigating this subject, I found many suggested prayers to use when consciously trying to offer up our suffering. My favorite was this one:[11]

> Dear Lord,
> Help me to remember in these troubled times
> The cross you carried for my sake,
> So that I may better carry mine
> And to help others do the same,
> As I offer up (whatever your concern or problem here) to you
> For the conversion of sinners
> For the forgiveness of sins
> In reparation for sins
> And for the salvation of souls.
> Amen.

Chapter 4
Finding Peace When You Do Want to Work

So you're a Catholic mother who works not because of financial necessity--or not only because of financial necessity--but because you feel a genuine calling from God to be his active instrument in the workplace, utilizing your intellect and gifts not only in your home, but in a professional capacity.

As it turns out, you're in excellent company! You aren't strange, or odd, or any "less" of a Catholic woman simply because you have discerned a secondary vocation in addition to your vocation as a wife and mother.

As Catholic women, we are called to use our diverse talents and gifts for the betterment of the Church, our family, and the world at large. Some of us are called by the Lord to use our talents solely within the sphere of the domestic church, but others are called to the mission field of the workplace. Consider how vastly different the calls of each of the saints were, and remember that you are just as unique.

In Scripture, Jesus made it clear that he expects us to use the talents he has bestowed upon us for the purpose of building up

> *"I have prayed about being called to my secondary vocation. It's hard when surrounded by women who stay at home and talk about homeschooling. But it comes down to the fact that I have been blessed with certain gifts, and I'm called to use those, which involves working out of the home. Plus, I'm a better mom when I work. It's not just about money sometimes. It's about mental health, burnout, anxiety, etc."*
>
> *— Kathryn W.*

the kingdom, instead of hiding them away (cf. Matthew 25:14-30). Through the Catholic Working Mothers Facebook group, I love seeing the varied ways Catholic women multiply the talents God gave them, and how they demonstrate to their children the ways their work — inside or outside the home — complements their vocation as a Catholic wife and mother.

I'd love to be able to share all of their stories with you; however, since my space is limited, I'm going to share interviews with six of my good friends. They are Catholic wives and mothers who also excel in the workplace, and who use their gifts to serve the Church and the world as well as their families.

Stacy's Story

Dr. Stacy Trasancos holds a PhD in chemistry from Penn State University and an MA in dogmatic theology from Holy Apostles College and Seminary. Currently, she works for the Saint Philip Institute of Catechesis and Evangelization founded by Bishop Joseph Strickland in the Diocese of Tyler, Texas. Formerly, she taught chemistry and physics for Kolbe Academy online homeschool program and served as the science department chair. She teaches chemistry and Reading Science in the Light of Faith at Holy Apostles College and Seminary, which is located in Cromwell, Connecticut. She is author of Science Was Born of Christianity: The Teaching of Fr. Stanley L. Jaki, 20 Answers — Bioethics, *and* Particles of Faith: A Catholic Guide to Navigating Science. *She is married and has seven children. Her website is http:// stacytrasancos.com/.*

I'm an educator, an author, a speaker, and a scientist. I left my position as a research chemist at DuPont to stay home with my kids. During that time, I started a blog and worked on an MA in dogmatic theology online. After I completed that degree, I began teaching online courses and writing books about theology and science, all from home. As the kids got older, I began doing some work outside the home. Looking back, I chose to do what I was passionate about, and found a way to turn it into a profession that grew with my kids. I found myself bored and anxious as five babies came along in a period of eight years. In addition, my oldest two teenagers were growing up, and I needed something to do to occupy my mind. I started studying theology at first because I was a new convert, and I wanted to learn more about my faith. But then I realized that people think there is a conflict between science and theology, so I used my knowledge of chemistry, biology, and physics, along with my new knowledge of theology, to start writing and teaching.

When I was trying to figure out what God wanted of me in the workforce, I practiced the virtue of prudence: the ability "to discern our true good in every circumstance and ... choose the right means of achieving it" (Catechism of the Catholic Church, 1806).

Josef Pieper, interpreting Saint Thomas Aquinas, describes four steps for practicing prudence: (1) silently contemplate reality; (2) be open-minded to receive instruction; (3) act swiftly with clear-sighted vision; and (4) fix the attention on what has not yet happened.[12] It means to think honestly and carefully when making decisions, and then to act knowing that you will constantly need to reassess. It's kind of like practicing the scientific method in life.

Motherhood and my profession are both aspects of who I am. Sometimes they mingle; sometimes I keep those parts of me completely separate. My job is to communicate effectively; being a mother has helped me to be more concise.

My job has also helped me to remember to think things through before answering my kids' questions; and, as they get older, it's fun to have deeper discussions with them. We make time for prayer by routine. We pray before meals. My husband and I walk in the mornings and pray the Rosary. We pray together as a family before bed. Personally, I talk to God a lot. In the mornings I pray for the grace to do God's will, because I need clarity to make good decisions. At night, I tell God I am his, to use me to lead souls to heaven. Sometimes I tell God what to do. "You HAVE to take care of my child!" Because I just don't know what else to pray for. Raising kids never gets easier.

My best advice for balancing work life, family life, and faith life is to make your days count. Work hard and do what you can, but also leave time for relaxation, play, and prayer. Don't worry too much about finding the sweet spot for balance. Just do what needs to be done.

Mary Elizabeth's Story

Mary Elizabeth Fabian is a small business owner who lives in Colorado. Most recently, she ran as a Republican candidate seeking election to the Colorado House of Representatives to represent District 18. She has been married to her husband for seventeen years and has three living children.

I work as an independent business consultant focusing on finance, growth, and media. I started this when I took a step back from full-time work. People who knew me professionally began seeking me out for consulting work. Basically, I fell into it. I felt the call in 2016, but I had previously worked for a handful of clients. I knew I needed to be home more and have flexible hours to assist in the care of my special-needs son. I was working sixty plus hours a week in intellectual property and loved it, but it was not conducive to my family's needs.

I constantly evaluate opportunities and growth within this area and others. I speak with my husband, friends who are familiar with my family dynamic, and a trusted priest. I know my earning power would be greater on a more traditional path, but this is where I am called today.

My vocation limits my willingness to accept additional clients and hours. It also makes me aware of the needs of other families, and I have been able to expand and offer other women positions where they can help meet the needs of their families. As I manage projects, I set deadlines, but I don't expect others to work my hours. I want a job done — when it's done is for them to decide.

I am able to show my daughters that I am empowered. I am capable on my own but willing to submit myself to a vocation and God's will, even when it's not my will.

Making time for prayer is hard for me. When I was a SAHM and a mom who worked outside the home, I had more time for devotions (meeting with other moms for prayer and Mass, or lunch breaks to focus on my spiritual growth). In my current situation, my prayers are said before I get out of bed in the morning and include few Hail Marys as I fall asleep. The rest is catch as catch can.

Not every family and work situation is the same. It is not necessary to measure ourselves by someone else's success or failures. We need to focus on what makes our careers, faith, and family live in harmony. No two families are the same.

Samantha's Story
Samantha Povlock has degrees in theology and business from the University of Notre Dame. She works as a project manager for a bank and is also the founder and creative director of FemCatholic (http://www.

femcatholic.com). She lives in the Chicago area. She has been married for three years and has two children.

I work for a bank doing project management finance as part of their Project Management Office. On the side I also run a platform called FemCatholic, which promotes new feminism and seeks to reconcile feminism and Catholicism.

I have always loved numbers, working with people, and organizing projects. In college, I majored in accounting, but then I worked in consulting because it allowed me more creativity and interaction with other people. I realized I really enjoy the combination of project management and finance, because it's a mix of everything I enjoy and where I can use my gifts.

In college I also majored in theology and had been feeling called to share my passion for women in the Church. After being accepted to a Catholic women's leadership conference called GIVEN, I had to create an action plan and follow through on it. FemCatholic was that action plan. I had so much doubt that I don't think I would have fully pursued it without the accountability of the GIVEN conference.

I knew that as the oldest of five kids, I was going to have to pay for college myself. After getting into the University of Notre Dame, I felt really strongly that I should go there, but also knew it would mean pursuing well-paying jobs after college to pay my loans. I'd been counseled to enter business, and it seemed like a good fit. Overall, it was the decision that brought me peace.

Some theology classes were also required for all students at Notre Dame, and I realized I received so much joy and insight from those classes. I filled the rest of my open credits with theology and was able to double major. Again, I felt a lot of peace about pursuing it — and I really enjoyed it!

An absolutely huge part of my discernment process has been talking with my husband — sharing our needs and stresses and vision for how our lives and family will grow. There are SO many intricate factors that play into a marriage and family that I wasn't aware of before getting married, and that I think many people leave out when they talk about working moms. There are considerations about personality type, finances — both present and in the future — extended family needs, dreams and passions, and number of children and their needs. These decisions are seasonal, too, because life and family are constantly changing!

I've reflected a lot on "what stresses me out," and "what fills me up." For whatever reason, I think I have been given the gift to go into an office every day, look at spreadsheets, and not feel totally burnt out by that. My own wonderful mom, who stayed home throughout my entire childhood, is the opposite: staying home with and caring for kids all day doesn't burn her out, but spreadsheets sure do! I think focusing on what allows you to be generous with yourself and your gifts is really important.

While most of the time my day job doesn't really "fill me up," my work for FemCatholic gives me so much joy and energy. I recently read Jennifer Fulwiler's book One Beautiful Dream, and the way she describes a "blue flame" passion — something that gives energy even when it requires time and effort — spoke to me so much. I've been involved in other extracurriculars before, but nowadays I really only have time for things that give me more energy — and FemCatholic does that.

Understanding myself as not just a mother, but as a whole person with a multifaceted vocation, has been enlightening. Like the Parable of the Talents, we're called to invest in all the gifts we've been given, and I recognize that I have been given gifts in both business and building an online platform. The idea of knowing a tree by its fruits has helped give me peace that I'm on the right path.

Most important was recognizing that our family has a vocation as a unit, too, and that we're all working together to best answer God's call and use our gifts as a team. It's not just all about me!

Being a mother has taught me so much about patience, and

> "I work part time as a pediatric occupational therapist, and I love my profession. I don't always love leaving my kids to go to work, but I am so happy that I am still able to use my talents as an OT. My children know that I go to work to help others, and because Mommy worked hard in school to learn how to be an OT. There is more than one way to be a great mom."
> — *Theresa C.*

perseverance, and priorities. That makes me more focused and intentional about the work I do, and the value I'm bringing in my job and to my team. I also think I'm better able to relate to people on a human level, especially fellow moms in the workplace.

My job in project management gives me space to exercise my mental muscles in a different way, so when I come home to my family I have more emotional energy to give and be present with them. It's also taught me some practical skills that I use to keep our household running! Overall, I think it makes me a much more peaceful and generous mom.

The joy my work with FemCatholic brings me overflows to my family. Raising kids takes a lot of effort, especially in a big city and without family very close by. This platform is an outlet that fills me up and helps me keep going, especially when things are busy and demanding.

I make time for prayer by playing a recording of the Rosary in the morning on the drive to daycare, and I'm trying to be better about praying throughout the day. I also get daily emails from Divine Mercy Daily, which I love. My husband and I go to daily Mass together once a week, too, during lunchtime.

My best advice for balancing work life, family life, and faith life is to believe that God has equipped you in a particular way for YOUR vocation, not anyone else's. He will give you the challenges, outlets, and hints along the way that speak to YOU. Don't second-guess that just because it doesn't look like someone else's situation. Follow what gives you peace, and hold on tight to that.

Deanna's Story

Deanna Johnston is a native of Memphis, Tennessee, and a current resident of Tyler, Texas. She graduated from the University of Memphis with a BA in philosophy and Spanish, and later earned her MA in theology from Newman University in Wichita, Kansas. She is a certified Billings Ovulation Method® NFP instructor. Currently, Deanna serves as the Director of Family Life for the Saint Philip Institute in the Diocese of Tyler. She has been married for five years, and she and her husband have three children (and one waiting for them in heaven).

Getting involved in marriage and family life ministry was inspired in part by the call to support the domestic church. Marriage is the foundation for the family, the family is the domestic church ... the "seedbed of vocations." Strong marriages lead to strong families, which leads to strong and vibrant parishes, which transform communities! I really enjoy working in an area that has the potential to impact society in such a powerful way.

Before I worked at the diocesan level, I spent several years working for a parish full time. While my job involved working with lots of different people in various situations, I was drawn primarily to ministries that allowed me to work with couples preparing for marriage and families. I think part of the inspiration behind working in family life ministry has also been the writings of Saint John Paul II, especially the Theology of the Body. It's a teaching that is helpful to so many spouses and families.

When I accepted my current position, it required us to move several hundred miles, so the discernment process was extremely important. First, it was not a position I would have accepted without enthusiastic encouragement from my husband. Second, my job allowed us to move much closer to both of our families, a situation that provided a system of support that we had never experienced before. We saw this as a major benefit, most especially to our children. Finally, and probably most importantly, there was a sense of peace about making this transition that we knew would only be possible if it was God's will.

I also know that the discernment process for determining God's will for my role in the workforce is an ongoing thing. There may very well come a time when I won't work full time, or God will call me to be a stay-at-home mom, and I need to be open to that. At this time, however, God is allowing me to use my gifts and talents both as a wife and mom and in full-time ministry.

My job is to help in the areas of marriage formation and marriage enrichment for couples and to also look at ways that we can support Catholic families in their particular season of life. Being a wife and a mom makes me passionate about the work that I do. I know that these ministries are needed, because my marriage and my family need support from the Church so that we can become saints!

Being a Catholic mother also allows me to bring a unique perspective to the workplace. I work with a lot of men, many of whom are priests. They are wonderful, holy, men of God, but there are times when having the feminine perspective, particularly as a wife and mother, allows me to contribute in ways that others cannot. The Church needs Catholic wives and moms to bring their "feminine genius" to the workplace!

One of the greatest blessings of my job is that it encourages me to "practice what I preach." As I'm leading retreats for engaged couples or working in marriage enrichment ministry, I'm often encouraging them to pray with their spouse, to make prayer and Mass a priority for their family, and to strive for holiness daily. I feel like I'm able to say from a place of honesty that doing these things is not always easy, but the ministry I'm involved in encourages me to keep working on my relationship with Christ so that I can be the wife and mom that I'm called to be.

However, making time for prayer is still an area I struggle with. One of the most helpful pieces of advice that a priest gave me recently when I shared my struggle was, "Pray as you can, not as you can't." My ideal prayer time might be sitting on the back porch in silence with my Bible and a cup of coffee while the sun rises over the pasture behind my house. But the reality is that my kids wake up ridiculously early, and trying to spend twenty minutes in quiet prayer before we leave for school and work is extremely difficult in our current season of life.

That being said, I'm learning to do what I can. Sometimes it means I pray with the kids on the way to school, take some time for prayer when I get to work, and then pray again at the end of the day with my family. Sometimes I'm able to go to daily Mass or spend time in adoration during my workday. I think the biggest lesson I'm learning is that it is much better to do something (whether that's five or ten minutes of quiet prayer instead of twenty to thirty) than to just blow off prayer completely because there "wasn't time." I can't be the wife and mom I'm called to be if I don't have a relationship with Jesus!

There is only peace and balance when relationships are in their proper order: God, spouse, children, and then work. This does not mean that I'm going to feel like Super Mom every day or that I won't feel frazzled from time to time. In my experience, I've seen that even in the busiest seasons, if God is first, then my relationships with my husband and my children are healthy and strong. As soon as work becomes more of a priority than taking time for prayer or my family life, things unravel quickly, and there is no peace. If God is first, then things are more ordered and balanced, both at home and at work!

Allicia's Story

Allicia Faber is a city girl transplanted to rural Arkansas. She has been married eight years and has three awesome kids: two daughters, ages eighteen months and six years, and a four-year-old son with Kool-en-de Vries Syndrome.

I'm currently a care team coordinator for a home health agency. What I do is basically a cross between a medical secretary and a scheduler. I fell into it when my parents opened a small private medical office. They asked me to help with the front office and billing, as I had some customer service and business writing experience. I worked for them until my first child was born. I was able to find work in the field even after we moved states.

I realized what my role in the workforce should be pretty quickly while working for my parents. Medicine is a calling for my dad; by seeing his approach to caring for others, I saw the way God was moving through the office.

I've taken leave from working a few times. Each time, my husband and I have discerned as a couple what the best course of action is — seeking guidance from prayer and reflection, talking it out with our families, and asking for advice from our priests. When we have been very conflicted, I've tried spending time in adoration, quietly listening for what God is trying to tell me. Each time I've taken a significant step back from work, as well as each time I've reentered the workforce, it has taken a lot of consideration in many ways.

I find that the values we hold as Catholics translate well to maintaining a good work ethic. Because I place a high value on the dignity of each person, I care deeply that we provide care that honors each person.

I've been blessed to find a job that allows me to drop my kids off at school every morning. I make time for prayer by listening to audio Rosaries and readings on my commute. When I manage to squeeze out time alone, I make rosaries as a hobby and use that time to pray.

It takes a lot of planning to make things run smoothly, so my advice is to schedule well. Make sure to include your prayer and reflection time in the week.

Amanda's Story

Amanda Martinez Beck is a Catholic author and size-dignity activist. She has a bachelor's degree in Spanish and religion and a master's degree in Spanish from Baylor University. She writes about being fat, Catholic, and loved at amandamartinezbeck.com and is the cohost of the Fat & Faithful podcast. She and her husband have been married for nine years and have four children ages six and under.

I have wanted to be a writer since I was a child, so when I got pregnant with my third child and was leaving my part-time job, I decided I would get serious about writing. I started telling other people that I was a writer, seeking out opportunities — unpaid at first — to write, and blogging on a regular basis. I've always loved writing, but when I was a freshman in college, a professor whom I admired was going over an exam I had written for him. He said I had a gift for writing. It wasn't much more than a comment of appreciation for my spontaneous writing skills — it was just an exam taken in fifty minutes — but it pressed itself into my heart. I thought I would be writing academically, because I had planned to get my PhD in Spanish literature after finishing up my master's in Spanish, but I found that telling stories made my heart come alive. That's where I am now, helping people see the stories that their bodies are telling.

When I was in graduate school, the thought occurred to me that God delights in cities. I thought, "Where would we be if architects hadn't used their sketching skills to build cities?" Every single part of a building has been touched by a human being, either literally or figuratively, and God delights when we put our creativity to both practical and impractical use.

I wondered what gifts I could use to build up other people, and I settled on storytelling and writing. It's the idea of a holistic stewardship: that our whole lives are part of our role as a steward in God's kingdom. That means that everything — not just my money — has an aspect of stewardship, including my writing gift and my storytelling gift. Also, I get to help people see their gifts and how they can steward them well.

My children ground me in reality. I could easily get caught up in my work, but they need my whole self — body and soul. The temptation to do a lot of thinking and mental work can be overwhelming for me at times. Their constant physical and emotional need for me roots me in the present moment. I love it. They help me tell stories better, because to be a good mom, I try to see things from their perspective. They are definitely responsible for a lot of the changes my body has gone through over the past seven years, which informs my work as a size-dignity activist. My body is good! They challenge me to accept and embrace that all the time.

One of my obsessions is consistency. I want everything I do to be consistent, so as I write and think through hard issues of faith, morals, and culture, I think about the story that I am showing to them — is it one of faithful and humble obedience to God my Father, and my mother the Church? Kids don't let you get away with hypocrisy, and my job has helped me slow down, analyze why I respond the way I do to specific things (like bodies and weight loss and comments about bodies), and lead them into faithfulness.

My favorite way to find time for prayer is the *Pray As You Go* podcast! On my hour-long commute, I set a timer of ten minutes for centering prayer, ten minutes for personal prayer, and ten minutes for husband and kids. I do lots of giving over of pain and suffering for specific intentions — one of my favorite things about being Catholic!

I have to recognize the line between my potential and my

capacity. Sure, I might have seven ideas that will make a million dollars (my potential), but do I have the time and resources to bring all of those ideas to fruition (my capacity)? When I resent my limited capacity as a wife and mother because I feel like my potential is foiled, I remind myself that my children and my husband expand my ability to do great things for Jesus. They teach me and stretch me and make me deepen my faith so that I can love them well, because that is my vocation.[13]

When I'm outside of Mass with my two little girls and don't hear the homily or anything else during the service, that actually increases my ability to come to Jesus

"[T]he world NEEDS mothers. And not just mothers at home, but mothers out in the world. In hospitals, in schools, in churches, in government, in businesses, etc. Mothers bring a special perspective, special experiences, and special skills. When we say that mothers should stay at home, we're basically only allowing a mother to shape her home environment, instead of other parts of society. Of course, a mother has to put her family before the rest of society. But if working is not detrimental, and she feels called to work, run for office, etc., then she should embrace that! I'd argue that our world is a sad and darker place because it has so often shunned women, including mothers, from having an equal impact."
— Rachel R.

as a little child — simply receiving him in the Eucharist, even though I wasn't able to pay attention to the rest of the Mass.

I hope you have benefited from the valuable advice and wisdom these women have so generously shared!

Pope Saint John Paul II has a wonderful message for the women who have vocations in the world as well as in the home:

> Thank you, women who work! You are present and active in every area of life — social, economic, cultural, artistic, and political. In this way you make an indispensable contribution to the growth of a culture which unites reason and feeling, to a model of life ever open to the sense of "mystery," to the establishment of economic and political structures ever more worthy of humanity.[14]

Perhaps Pope Saint John Paul II was thinking of Saint Gianna Molla when he penned those words. Her mission to care for her neighbors, body and soul, did not end when she became a wife and mother. Per her husband, Pietro Molla:

> Gianna chose medicine in the belief that more than any other professions, it would permit her to help many people in body and spirit. Besides, this profession is based on interpersonal relationships, to which Gianna was much inclined. In her manuscripts she says precisely that a doctor has opportunities closed even to the priest. In her view, a doctor has to care not only for the body, but also for the soul. Thus, she conceived the profession as a mission. […] For Gianna, the choice of medicine also meant continuing her commitment to the service of neighbor, as she had learned in her family and had done in the apostolate with young women in Catholic Action.[15]

Similarly, as Saint Edith Stein acknowledged:

> Wherever the circle of domestic duties is too narrow for the wife to attain the full formation of her powers, both nature and reason concur that she reach out beyond this circle.[16]

How bereft the Church and the world would be without the many Catholic women who have used their feminine genius in the workplace! Thank you for contributing your talents for the building up of the kingdom, even as you oversee the domestic church within your home.

Chapter 5

Tools for Discernment

My favorite movie of all time is *The Sound of Music*. I've probably watched it a hundred times. It has the perfect storm of movie elements: musical song-and-dance numbers, Julie Andrews, and nuns. (And, let's face it: Captain von Trapp is a dreamboat.) I also love that the real Maria von Trapp was a Catholic working mother! Along with her family, she was an entertainer who toured worldwide, and later she helped run a music camp in Vermont. Throughout her life, she remained devoted to her Catholic Faith.

The movie also provides a wonderful description of discernment. Early on in the film, the Mother Superior of the convent calls Maria into her office and asks her, "What is the most important lesson you have learned here, my child?"

Maria answers, "To find out what is the will of God and … to do it wholeheartedly."

Discernment is the first part of that equation — to find out what is the will of God. With some issues, this is fairly easy. We know from the teaching of the Church that it is the will of God that we attend Mass, that we regularly make use of the Sacrament of Reconciliation, that we take the Eucharist, that we do not kill, that we do not commit adultery, and so on.

But with other issues, the will of God is not so clear. Maria thought she had discerned a call to religious life; but her spiritual director, the Mother Superior, helped her discern otherwise. She had to leave the convent and serve as a governess for the von Trapp family in order to fully discover God's will for her life. Even then, there were bumps along the way before she realized she was being called to the vocation of marriage and family (and later, a career as an entertainer) instead of religious life.

There often are several paths we can take in the course of our lives — for example, choosing to work outside the home, or quitting a full-time job to work part time from home — and while they may point in different directions, each one of them conforms to the teaching of the Church. Or perhaps God's will happens to be radically different than what we had planned for our lives, and he surprises us. The Blessed Virgin Mary was lucky enough to get a clear message from God, via the angel Gabriel, that changed the course of her life — likely one that radically diverged from the direction she had anticipated.

But most of us aren't lucky enough to get our Angel Gabriel. Sometimes God gives us clear signs and signals to indicate which path we should choose; but sometimes his will is not clearly evident, and we need to seek out that knowledge for ourselves.

Why does God want us to discern his will, instead of sending us an angel to tell us what to do? There are two reasons: (1) he wants to respect our free will, which includes giving us the option to *reject* his will; and (2) through the process of discernment, he wants us to grow closer to him.

Every major decision — and even some minor ones — in our lives should be a result of careful and comprehensive discernment, and employment decisions are no exception. As I discussed in chapter 4, the work we do is not always merely a means to an end (i.e., providing for our family); it can be a secondary vocation as well.

The discernment of our vocation is never a one-time event, but rather a continuous process that lasts as long as we are alive and capable of serving God in any capacity. We may know what our vocation is in a general sense — for example, we may know that we are called to marriage and family instead of religious life — but we must also discern how, where, and with whom we should fulfill our specific vocation.

Once we have fulfilled the initial objectives of our primary vocation, our discernment changes to how best to live our vocation: to discover God's will within the context of our vocation, and then to do his will wholeheartedly.

As a Catholic working mother, you may have discerned your secondary vocation as a working professional prior to marriage. Once you married, or preferably during the marriage preparation process, you discerned what your secondary vocation would look like in the context of your primary vocation as a wife and mother. This is a discernment that should and will be often repeated in your life as the size and circumstances of your family change.

> *"Some women thrive at home being with their kids all the time. Some women think they should be home but are totally miserable. Some working moms thrive at work and come home energized to give their children lots of attention and affection. Some working moms feel defeated and go home too tired to invest in their kids. A thriving mom is more effective than a miserable mom. There's no cookie-cutter way to be a mom — the best we can offer our kids is reviewing our own family dynamics and choosing the best fit for us."*
> *— Danielle O.*

Three Aspects to Thorough Discernment

In general, there are three aspects to thorough discernment, which I have dubbed the "Three Eyes" (Eyes = I's ... get it?): Information, Invocation, and Intuition.

1. INFORMATION

God gave human beings intelligence and reason, and we should make use of both those gifts in the discernment process. In order to evaluate your options, you need hard data about the benefits and disadvantages of each choice.

In my experience, there are three key areas of your family life to analyze when discerning employment possibilities, whether you are considering working outside the home for the first time, evaluating a job change, or exploring the transition to stay-at-home parent:

- Finances
- Health (physical, spiritual, mental, and emotional)
- Logistics

The example questions I've included below are by no means exhaustive, but they provide a good framework for what you should consider in each aspect of your family life.

Finances

To analyze your family's finances, you need to know:

Your family's household budget. Is the amount of income that you'll bring home after childcare, taxes, and health insurance premiums (if applicable) significant or negligible? If the amount is negligible, is the health insurance a factor that makes working worth it, regardless? (For some families with intensive medical needs, it may be worth working just to have good health insurance, even if actual earned income isn't a large amount. Medical debt can be significant and is a leading cause of bankruptcy.)

Your family's debt-to-income ratio. Are two incomes necessary just to keep on top of the bills? Will two incomes help pay down debt faster (which might allow one of you to transition to being a stay-at-home parent at a later time)? Will a new job put your family into debt (due to the need to purchase another vehicle, or something similar)?

Your family's current and future financial goals. Have you and your husband worked out a retirement plan? Can you afford life insurance policies for each of you in case one of you dies prematurely, and/or life insurance policies for your children to cover funeral costs if the worst happens? Do you plan to invest in college funds for your children? Do you plan on budgeting for Catholic school once your children are school-aged? Are you saving for a down payment on a house? Are you trying to pay off your mortgage or cars early?

The potential expenses involved with a job transition. Sometimes there are "hidden costs" involved with working that you may forget to factor into your budget. Childcare is the biggest and most obvious cost, but there are also fuel costs for your commute as well as wear-and-tear on your vehicle, or the cost of public transportation to and from work.

There may be an additional food cost; even if you bring your lunch to work every day, there's always the occasional lunch out with coworkers, or a fast-food run if it was a hectic morning and you forgot your lunch, or you unexpectedly work late and need to grab a quick supper on the way home.

Another expense to consider is wardrobe; dress code can vary from office to office, and you need to evaluate and factor in the cost of new clothing purchases, if needed, or uniform costs if required by your employer.

Health
Health concerns are also important to analyze — not just physical health, but also mental, emotional, and spiritual health.

Physical health. Are your family's medical needs such that you need excellent health insurance? Are you able to work outside the home physically, or do you have chronic pain or fatigue? Do you anticipate any future health needs that would preclude you from working? Are your pregnancies generally easy, or do you suffer from medical conditions that might affect your ability to work? Do your children have specific health needs that might make a full-time job difficult to maintain? Does your spouse have health concerns that currently or might someday affect his ability earn income?

Mental/emotional health. Will the stress of working full time or part time negatively affect your mental health? Does the stress of staying at home full time caring for children negatively affect your mental health? Do you have therapy needs that a new job could inhibit, or might make affordable? Will a new job help you to afford medication for a mental-health condition that would otherwise be too expensive? Will gaining a new job or leaving a current job affect the health of your marriage? Do your children have mental- or emotional-health needs that cannot be met by another caregiver at this time?

Spiritual health. Will a new job cause strain on your family's spiritual health by making it more stressful and difficult to find time for family prayer or attending Mass or religious education? Will gaining a new job or leaving a current job positively or negatively affect your family's ability to tithe your time, talent, and treasure? Will it be a problem to live your faith as a Catholic in this position — could you be asked to compromise your moral beliefs, especially if they don't conform to those of secular culture?

Logistics

What does your family's current schedule look like? Will one spouse have to bear the brunt of pickups and drop-offs, or can you equally split those responsibilities? Who will be responsible for running errands if both parents are working full time? How will housework be divided? Who will help the kids with homework at night?

Will either parent have the flexibility to leave work or take several days off work if a child becomes ill? Are there medical appointments or therapy that must take precedence over a work schedule? Will one parent be able to take children to well-child exams as needed?

Do one or both spouses have an extensive commute or an excessively heavy schedule that might eat into family time? Is there significant out-of-town travel involved for one or both spouses? How much vacation time does each spouse receive? Does either spouse have the flexibility to work from home or take time off to stay at home to wait for a plumber or exterminator or repair personnel, when needed?

There are probably a dozen more questions in each category that you could ask. Each family's situation and circumstances are unique, and in order to fully evaluate all of the advantages and disadvantages of an employment decision, you need to gather as much information as possible and thoroughly analyze all the ways your decision could affect your family's life. If the "cons" list of your potential situation far outweighs the "pros" list, that could be one way in which God is showing you his will.

2. INVOCATION

To seek the will of God, you must communicate with him using the means he has given us for that purpose: prayer, worship, and contemplation. More importantly, you must *listen*, and be receptive to hearing what he is telling you — even if his answer isn't the one you were hoping for.

Also brace yourself for the possibility that God's response to your prayers might be completely unexpected, or cause major upheaval in your life. For example, when I was discerning whether to write this book and submit the proposal to Our Sunday Visitor, I prayed a novena to Saint Gianna Beretta Molla, asking for her intercession. Specifically, I prayed that if it was God's will for me to write this book, that he would help me find the time to write it amid working full time and riding herd over six children.

The same week that I submitted my book proposal, I was quite abruptly laid off from my full-time job ... *and* my husband was offered a new job that came with a significant salary increase, one that made it possible for me to stay at home full time and focus on writing my book instead of immediately having to seek another full-time job. It was an unexpected but very unmistakable answer to my novena.

Another time, my husband and I were discerning whether to move across the country to pursue better job opportunities, as the economy in the area in which we lived was not promising. We prayed separately and together, and both of us asked God to remove specific obstacles in our path if it was his will that we move away from our current home.

Our obstacles (which involved finding a new renter for our apartment so that our current landlord would let us out of our lease with no penalties, as well as finding the money to rent a moving truck) were cleared within two weeks, and we were able to make the move shortly thereafter.

> "When I am struggling to see the right path, my prayer is always for God to make straight the paths that go before me. I also take great comfort in meditating on the Glorious Mysteries and that he has already fought the good fight, won, and went ahead to prepare a place for us ... leaving us the Holy Spirit to guide us to his father and his mother to remind us of our royal family and heritage we have not earned but been given as a gift."
> — Kim T.

Prayer

Prayer is essential during the discernment process. Pray constantly about your situation, specifically asking God to help you in making a decision that conforms to his will. Pray also to the Holy Spirit, asking for wisdom and guidance.

The Rosary is a powerful prayer, and there are many novenas specifically geared toward discernment, as well as ones that directly relate to asking for intercession with job-related situations and concerns. You can find a list of my favorites as well as other tools for discernment in appendix 1.

Worship

In addition to attending Mass on Sundays, try to attend daily Mass. If not possible, try to find time to stop by your parish or any nearby Catholic church and pray. It's easier to focus our prayers when we have an environment conducive to prayer and worship, and a church or chapel is the best place for that.

Adoration of the Holy Eucharist is also helpful in the discernment process. If you have an adoration chapel nearby, or if your parish has a set time for adoration, try to fit in as much time as you can manage to pray in front of the Blessed Sacrament, or to simply sit in the presence of Jesus and *listen* to what he may be telling you.

Contemplation

It may be difficult if you are facing a time-sensitive situation, but attending a Catholic spiritual retreat where you can fully focus on prayer and worship for a few days can be very beneficial when discerning an important life change. One of the members of the CWM Facebook group said, "I did this once, and it revealed to me some powerful things that made me open to the way my career naturally evolved; I would have for sure fought God had I not gone on this particular retreat."

Seeking advice from a trusted Catholic friend, orthodox

> "Saint Joseph and Our Lady of Knots are my two go-tos for discernment. Another one is to follow the Ignatian discernment steps."
>
> — Marlo V.

spiritual advisor, or holy priest is also beneficial. We have many women who ask questions relating to their discernment in the CWM Facebook group, as a way to help ensure that they've fully explored all aspects of their situation; they also ask the other members to pray for them as they discern.

A self-guided retreat — going alone to a nearby convent, monastery, or retreat center, or even just spending the night in a hotel room or at a relative's house by yourself, focusing on prayer — could be helpful if you are struggling with a decision and need some time or space alone to think things through.

3. INTUITION

All the data you have might be pointing in one direction, but what if your intuition is pointing in another direction? What is your gut telling you? What is your conscience saying? Are the fruits of the Holy Spirit — love, joy, peace, forbearance, kindness, goodness, faithfulness, gentleness, and self-control — present in your decision-making process?

Do you have a bad feeling about a job offer even though, on paper, it looks good? Do you have peace about a particular decision even though you're not quite sure how the logistics or finances will work out? Are your heart and your head giving you conflicting messages?

Do listen to your conscience, but make sure the voices in your head aren't unduly influenced by secular culture or unorthodox Catholic teaching.

Discerning one's employment situation is quite similar to discerning one's family size: Only the couple themselves, in the sight of God, can discern what best fits their family's situation. Only they know the intimate details of their mental health, physical health, financial situation, and household concerns, so only they can make the call as to what their working dynamics, both individually and as a couple, should look like. It's never a bad idea to seek guidance from a faithful spiritual director or priest; but in the end, the decision can only be yours.

Remember, employment decisions aren't necessarily permanent. If circumstances allow, you could make the decision to try a new job for three months, and at that time reevaluate how your job is affecting your family's health, finances, and so on. Or, if you want to quit your job to stay at home with your children, try living on one income for three months while putting your paycheck in your savings, and see whether it is manageable.

Be at peace knowing that even if you make the wrong choice, God can bring good out of it, or use the consequences of your decision for your greater good. He will not abandon us if we make poor choices, and he will always give us the grace we need to get back on the right path.

Chapter 6

Home Management

I am the very last person who should be writing this chapter, because I am a hot mess when it comes to home management. I have entirely too much clutter; my attempts at meal planning are hit or miss; and I hate housework. When I worked full time outside the home, what I hated most was trying to figure out how to get all of those tasks done. Even now, as a quasi-work-from-home-mom, I still struggle.

However, this book has emerged not only from my experiences but also those of all the moms in the CWM Facebook support group. So I'm going to take a stab at sharing the different strategies our members have employed, and hopefully you can find one that works for you and your family.

Because every family has unique circumstances, schedules, needs, and priorities, every family's strategy for home management will be different — there is no one-size-fits-all solution. All you can do is try to figure out what works for you and your family. It's often going to be crazy and hectic, and there are never going to be enough hours in the day to get it all done.

It's interesting to note that fathers aren't often asked how they manage to balance their jobs with family life and housework. The assumption seems to be that women are going to take care of all

> *"Balance is hard! No husband, so it's just me and the kids. I try to find as many life hacks as I can. I order online groceries during my lunch break, then just pick up. I've found a friend who cleans my house once a month for a reasonable price; a local teen takes care of my yard; one sport for the kids, so drop-off and pickup is the same time. Even my toddlers have to help keep things clean and picked up — a pack survives together. My biggest life hack is to seriously limit how much stuff we have. Less clothes, less toys equals less stuff to clean and pick up."*
> *— Beth L.*

that. But when both parents work, the division of labor needs to be equal. It can't all be on one person — and even if the mother works full time while the father stays home, he needs help too. It's too big a job for one person to handle. (Single mothers, you have my undying respect and admiration, because I have no idea how you manage solo.)

A frequent topic of discussion in the CWM group is how to get husbands to pitch in when it comes to housework and childcare. If you can, set expectations early on in your marriage, before kids come along. If both spouses are working, both need to contribute equally to the household tasks. It isn't always going to be equal; there may be seasons when the split is off-balance due to illness, pregnancy, an important work deadline or business trip, etc. But on average, each spouse should be carrying an equal load. Parenting is a full-time job too, and a mother or father who works needs to be equally committed to both jobs, and not simply another child who needs to be parented and catered to by his or her spouse.

If expectations haven't been set, call a family meeting and

work together to create a plan. Don't lecture, criticize, or nag; treat it as a business meeting with a peer. Work together to brainstorm the essential tasks that need to get done, and delegate who does what according to personal strengths and preferences.

I've found that the best strategy is to prioritize. Decide what aspect of your home life will drive you absolutely insane if it doesn't get done, and try not to worry about the rest. In my experience, this breaks down into three main areas of home management: cleaning and decluttering/organizing, meal planning, and laundry/clothes management.

It is a proven fact that clutter causes anxiety,[17] so this is a key source of stress for lots of working moms, especially those with many young kids. For others, they feel most on top of things if they have meals prepped and ready to go. Others need to stay on top of the laundry in order to feel in control. If not having all three done regularly is killing you, it might be wise to try to lower your standards and give yourself some grace.

Cleaning and Decluttering

Did I mention that I hate housework? Unfortunately, I married a fellow slob, so our house is in a constant state of chaos and clutter. Every so often we make an effort to do better, and sometimes we succeed, but those instances are few and far between. Yet I still manage to keep things running, after a fashion. Now that our oldest children are able to help out, things have improved. Still, we have a long way to go.

My biggest advice for cleaning: HIRE HELP. I cannot emphasize this enough. If you can afford it — which, admittedly, is a big *if* — have someone come in at least once every two weeks and do general cleaning — mopping floors, vacuuming, cleaning bathrooms, and maybe even finishing up dishes. My husband and I were able to afford this at one point when we were both working full time, and it was SUCH a stress reliever for us —

especially while I was pregnant, and it was all I could do to drag myself to and from work every day and keep the kids fed and clean. Unfortunately, we had to give up the housecleaning service once our daycare costs rose too high, and we haven't been able to fit it back in the budget yet.

Alternatively, there are high-tech gadgets available. Some CWM members swear by their robot mops and vacuums, although I hear they may not be a good idea if you have pets. Still, if dirty floors drive you nuts, you may want to look into one or both gadgets, or ask for them (or gift cards toward their purchase) for Christmas or birthday gifts.

I am following (or trying to follow) some of the guidelines given by Dana White at A Slob Comes Clean (aslobcomesclean .com). Her books are written for people like me with "slob vision," and she has a blog and a podcast that I find helpful as well. Other moms in the CWM group have had luck with systems like Flylady (Flylady.net), Messies Anonymous (messies.com), or the book *Organizing Solutions for People with ADHD* by Susan Pinsky.

I have also sought advice from Catholic working mother Sterling Jaquith, author of *Not of This World: A Catholic Guide to Minimalism.* I asked her for her best advice for Catholic working mothers when it comes to practicing minimalism, and she told me the following:

> I can't stand clutter. Even before I read the statistics about how clutter in your home causes real stress and anxiety, I knew it was bad for me. One moment I'd finally get the house clean, and a few hours later, my circus of five kids would come through like a tornado of socks, books, toys, and papers. Oh, so many papers!
>
> There are all sorts of challenges out there to help you get rid of the stuff in your home that you don't need, but let me tell you a secret: You don't need to overthink this. There are three things I do to routinely evict unwanted stuff

from my house and to keep my home tidy and picked up.

Designated Spot

I have a spot in my house where I continually toss things that I intend to donate. When I come across something I don't want, I put it in that spot … it's a chair actually. Now my kids even understand what this space means, and I get some protesting when they find things they like in the chair. But they know me by now. If it's in the chair, it's heading out of the house!

Closest Thrift Store

Find the thrift store closest to your house or one that is on the way to a place you go often, like church or the grocery store. Begin training yourself: *When I leave to get groceries, I'm going to stop by the thrift store on the way.* Most of these places allow you to drive up, hand them a few bags and continue on your way. If you're a busy lady, stop telling yourself that you're going to sell things. I PROMISE, the peace you're going to get by getting rid of that clutter is worth way more than the ten dollars (plus the hassle) of selling something on Craigslist.

Quick Tidy

The last thing I do isn't so much about getting rid of stuff as it is about the cleaning of spaces so my house looks tidy. I have discovered that when enough clutter piles up on my dresser, the kitchen counter, and the dining room table, my anxiety thermometer starts to climb! Twice a day at my house, we have a five-minute pickup! I usually put on a fun song, and everyone has to relocate things that have accumulated in public spaces back to where the things ought to go. We say, "Put this back in its home." Though this is no substitute for minimizing how much you own, it will help your sanity in the meantime as you continue your journey to live with less!

Ladies, your peace is worth more than you can imagine. Maintaining peace is the key to becoming a saint. Nothing is worth stealing your peace. Just keep asking yourself that about each item that you own. Is this stealing my peace? Why do I need it? Slowly but surely, you'll cultivate a home that brings you peace instead of anxiety.

Jaquith's book is worth reading because it is chock-full of more excellent advice along those lines, and I highly recommend it for those working hard to simplify their lives and get rid of the stuff that we all seem to surround ourselves with.

There is no magic bullet, but sometimes you can find a strategy or strategies that work for you and add them to your routine.

Give yourself a reward while doing it (or even after doing it). Folding laundry can be a great excuse for a Netflix binge. Doing the dishes or mopping the floors is an opportunity to listen to your favorite podcasts or an audiobook.

Divvy up chores according to who hates what the least. My husband hates loading the dishwasher but doesn't mind unloading it, and I don't care either way. I hate clearing the table and putting the leftovers away after I've cooked dinner, so my husband does that chore for me. I hate scrubbing toilets less than he does, so generally I do that, too, and he does 100 percent of the bill paying because math gives me a headache.

If you have older kids, make daily chores part of their routine. You can tie this to an allowance or earning screen time or so on, depending on your parenting philosophy and your kids' temperaments. I somehow managed to give birth to a daughter, now fourteen, who both enjoys cleaning *and* does a good job. (I think she gets that from her grandmother, because she didn't get it from me!) She helps a lot around the house, and as a result she earns extra privileges that her younger siblings don't have.

Finally, sometimes a change of perspective can help. I often ruminate on the words I read several years ago in an article on CatholicMom.com by Patrice Fagnant-MacArthur:

> Housework is an opportunity to encounter God. ... Every moment of our lives, if offered to God and done to serve him, is holy. That includes the time spent with the laundry or scrubbing the floor. First of all, we do these things because they are part of our vocation, and one of our primary duties on this earth is to serve God by living our vocation to the best of our abilities. Secondly, we do our housework to serve those we love — so that they may have clean dishes and clean clothes and a healthy environment to live in. It may not seem that way as we are struggling to get it done, but doing the housework is actually an act of love.[18]

There are some seasons of life when you need to operate in survival mode. This is a concept I first read about on Jennifer Fulwiler's blog. (If you Google her name plus "survival mode," the first few results are several of her posts on this subject.) She defines these times as "seasons of life when things are too crazy to do anything other than just get by."

I've found that these seasons usually accompany sources of great transition or turmoil — a pregnancy (especially the first trimester, when I'm constantly sick and exhausted, and the last month or two, when I feel too big to move off the couch), a new baby, a toddler in a particularly destructive phase, a child who has a serious illness or who has been diagnosed with special needs, a new and demanding job, a parent or relative who is seriously ill, the start of a new school year, and so on.

These are the times when you do the bare minimum necessary

to keep everyone clothed and fed — even if that means the kids get more screen time than usual. Even if that means the house stays in a state of chaos for a while. Even if that means saying no to some outside commitments or volunteer activities. Even if that means increasing your budget for takeout food or a babysitter or house-cleaner for a while.

But above all, do not make perfect the enemy of good. If I don't have time to mop the kitchen floor perfectly, that's okay — as long as it gets somewhat clean. If my husband doesn't fold the towels perfectly, that's okay — as long as clean towels are in the linen closet for us to use. If your child cleans the bathroom and the toilet bowl isn't spotless, at least it's better than it was.

Aim for progress, not perfection, because that's a much easier standard to achieve.

The same is true with decluttering. Again, I highly recommend Sterling Jaquith's book about Catholicism and minimalism, because she has great practical tips as well as spiritual insights regarding the art and virtues of practicing simplicity. I've also found a lot of helpful strategies in Dana White's book *Decluttering at the Speed of Life: Winning Your Never-Ending Battle with Stuff* and on her website (mentioned above).

My advice is to start small. Aim for one box or garbage bag per week if that's all you can manage (and if you can do more, good for you).

If your clutter problem is really bad — we're talking a *Hoarders*-level mess that makes your home hazardous or unsafe — it might not be a bad idea to hire a professional. There's no shame in seeking help if clutter is overwhelming your life. Do a Google search for "hoarding help," and you'll find many resources.

Meal Planning

I actually enjoy meal planning. *Sticking* to the plan is another story altogether, but I do like the planning part. Like cleaning and decluttering, there are myriad tools, methods, services, and strategies for meal planning, so the key is to find one that plays to your strengths or that fits into your existing schedule. Some people like having a binder with all of their recipes. Some people like using a daily planner and scheduling their meals there. Others prefer technology-based tools and use an electronic service or website or app.

I fit into the latter category. I've turned Pinterest into my main recipe repository, and my boards are even somewhat organized. When I do meal plan (which, admittedly, is fast and loose these days), I do a quick inventory of my fridge, freezer, and pantry, and then search for recipes on my boards that use the ingredients I have or want to use up. If I find one that works, I pin it to a board called "Meal Plan" and refer to it during the week.

If you're in survival mode, I have found it is best to stick with the same set of recipes — say, seven to ten different meals — and just rotate them. If it helps to have the same meal on each day of the week, do that. Sure, it may seem monotonous, but sometimes the routine is what you need when you are just trying to make it through the day (or week, or month). It simplifies your grocery list and your to-do list in terms of trying to figure out what to make and when to prepare it.

So, you might do spaghetti on Mondays, tacos on Tuesdays, pork chops on Wednesdays, chicken on Thursdays, pizza on Fridays, burgers on Saturdays, and pot roast on Sundays. Once you're out of survival mode, then you can experiment a bit and branch out. (If anyone complains, they can take over cooking for a while!)

Many members of the CWM group have had luck with services such as eMeals or The Dinner Daily, because they do the meal planning. I've done trials of both services in the past, and I can see how they could be helpful, but they didn't work for me because of the size of my family (most of the services max out at plans for families of four to six, and we have eight), as well as the preferences of some of my picky eaters (including me).

Some like the "once a month cooking method," where you spend one weekend day per month cooking enough freezer meals to last you for thirty days. This only works if you have the room in your budget to do a month's worth of grocery shopping at once, though, and the freezer space to hold all the meals. You can also do this on a weekly basis. I've never been able to achieve consistency with it, but your mileage may vary.

Regarding grocery shopping, see whether any of your area stores offer online ordering and curbside pickup. I started doing this months ago, and it has *changed my life*. Grocery shopping is so much easier now! I can build my list in bits and pieces, adding items to my cart on the store's smartphone app whenever I have a spare moment, or whenever someone says, "Hey, we're out of ___." or "we need more ___." Once my order is ready, I schedule a pickup time at my convenience (for example, right after I get off work), and when I arrive at the store, my order is loaded into the car for me — I don't even have to get out of the car! It's made grocery shopping so much easier and more convenient, and it's well worth the five-dollar fee.

If your area doesn't provide this service, or if your favorite store doesn't offer it, try to turn grocery shopping into a minivacation on the weekends. Leave the kids at home with your husband, get a latte, and take your time wandering the aisles with your favorite music playing in your earbuds. Or, if you have more than one child, use it as an opportunity to get some one-on-one time with a particular kid. Age permitting, give him or her a list to hunt down items for you — to some kids, grocery shopping is a super fun scavenger hunt. If your husband enjoys grocery shopping but you don't, delegate that task to him. Or, make it a family event on the weekends so that at least you have someone there to share the burden and help rein in the little ones.

I really recommend budgeting for an Amazon Prime subscription, if possible. I like using Amazon Prime's subscription service for many consumables — toilet paper, paper towels, giant boxes of cleaning sponges, and so on. Those supplies are automatically ordered and magically appear at my door without me having to think about it. If I forget something in my grocery order that isn't crucial immediately but that I'll need in the next few days, or if my child suddenly remembers on Tuesday night that she needs a Molly Pitcher costume for her social studies presentation on Friday (yes, that actually happened), Amazon Prime and two-day shipping to the rescue!

My favorite cooking gadget for working moms is an electric pressure cooker (mine is an Instant Pot), a device that cooks food by heating liquid to boiling, which forms steam within a sealed pot. The steam cooks the food rapidly and forces liquid into it, which increases moisture and helps quickly tenderize cuts of meat. Once it's done cooking, you vent the steam out of the pot through a valve on the top. Using one requires a bit of a learning curve at first, but once you learn the ropes, a whole new world of cooking possibilities opens up for you.

Why are they so great for working mothers? Two words: They're fast. You can cook an entire pot roast in ninety minutes, start to finish. Something like macaroni and cheese takes around ten minutes from scratch (and it's so much better than the boxed stuff). When I make honey teriyaki chicken, it's usually done cooking in the pressure cooker before my rice is complete. This magical device can cook a meal in less than an hour *even if your meat is frozen.*

My rice cooker and my slow cooker are also indispensable. You might want to explore air fryers and large electric griddles, too.

Just remember: For weeknight meals, or meals on days when you work, keep it simple. One-pot meals are best so you don't have a lot of dishes to clean up. If you enjoy cooking more elaborate meals, save them for the weekends or holidays. Speed and efficiency are what work best on busy nights when there are only a few hours between arriving home and bedtime. Ask other working moms for their meal plans; you might get a few tips and recipes you didn't have before.

Laundry and Clothes Management

Laundry

The real never-ending story isn't about a ten-year-old and a giant dragon; it's about laundry. Pants, shirts, dresses, baby clothes, underwear, lingerie, pajamas, bath towels, sheets, mattress covers, pillow cases, blankets, dish towels, washcloths, even stuffed toys ... it never ends. Toss in an infant who spits up two or three times a day, or a toddler who loves to strip naked on a regular basis, or a teen who changes clothes six times a day, and it's enough to drive you mad.

CWMs employ several different strategies for getting the laundry done. Some swear by doing a load every day: Put a load in the washing machine in the morning before work; immediately switch it over to the dryer once you get home; and fold and put it away once the kids are in bed. Or put in a load right away when you get home, switch it to the dryer immediately after supper, and fold and put it away before bed.

Others like to let the laundry pile up over the week and tackle it all at once over the weekend. Some prefer to take it all to a laundromat on the weekends so they can do multiple loads at once. (This can get expensive, but it isn't a bad solution if you're already in an apartment building with coin-operated machines.)

Or, as I've been known to do, you can wait until various family members are stressed and upset because no one has anything to wear, and then do an emergency load that ends up sitting in a basket for weeks while adults and kids alike dig through it looking for clothes. Once the basket is empty, it's time for another emergency load!

I had a system going for a while where I had a white plastic laundry hamper labeled with each person's name. (I used a Sharpie.) I even put pictures on the kids' hampers for the benefit of those who couldn't read yet. I nagged the kids incessantly about putting their dirty clothes in "their" hamper, and for a few weeks it worked well — if someone needed clothes to wear, I'd go get the hamper and do a load (or, age permitting, they did it themselves). But once I stopped nagging, it all fell apart, and somehow the hampers migrated all around the house. Still, it was a fairly good system while it lasted.

> "Every night we pick up before bed. Sometimes it's everyone; sometimes it's just me. I make sure the living room is picked up, blankets and pillows fluffed, toys in the play room, kitchen cleaned. Then, each morning, we put dirty clothes away and make all the beds. I do all my real cleaning on the weekends. I think the key is just trying to tidy once a day!"
>
> *— Julie Z.*

Here are a couple of tips that have helped me stay sane, if not organized, with laundry:

- I don't sort clothes by type; I only sort them by person. I wash everything on cold. We own very few items of clothing that need to be hand-washed or dry-cleaned (and those we do own are things like Christmas dresses and my husband's three-piece suit ... items that don't need to be cleaned often).

- I do wash towels and sheets separately, but sometimes I'll throw in a towel or two along with a load of clothes if we're running low, which buys me some time until I have the chance to do a full load of towels.

• If I could do it all over again, I would only buy the same brand and color of socks for each kid, but I didn't start out that way. Now, we are drowning in socks. As a result, I stopped caring about matching socks a *long* time ago. As long as the kid in question has two clean socks on, I call it good. If someone comments about their mismatched socks, I proudly brag about my child's unique method of expressing their individuality. Or I invite the person to come over and spend a few hours with my sock basket.

• I have sent kids to school with mismatched shoes if one shoe has mysteriously gone missing — I figure it's more important that they go to school with two mismatched shoes than stay at home. Since I put a shoe rack near our front door and nagged everyone to use it, this happens less often, although my five-year-old seems to have a special gift for losing one of his shoes on a regular basis.

• I don't have a good place in my front foyer for a large rack or hooks, so I put a large plastic tote near the front door, next to the shoe rack, and they all throw their backpacks in the tote when they get home. (Coats go in there during the cooler months as well.) That minimizes the frantic cries of "Mom, I can't find my backpack!" in the mornings when we're rushing around trying to get out the door.

• Another strategy recommended by Dana White of *A Slob Comes Clean* is to always fold or hang laundry as you are taking it out of the dryer, and immediately put the clothes away. She says this minimizes the temptation to throw it on a loveseat or bed with the mentality of "I'll put it away later" ... and then find it still there three weeks later. This is a work in progress for me, but I will admit it is effective when I have the time and space to do so.

• Laundry should be a family effort! If you have older kids, draft them as laundry helpers. Make a big deal out of how helping with the laundry is a rite of passage. Even little ones (ages four and five) can put folded clothes into a drawer. They're going to have to do their own laundry eventually, so the earlier they start, the better. They can help fold and put away; eventually, they can be in charge of doing their own laundry. (The key here is to totally ignore it when, for example, they are wearing jeans and a sweater on a ninety-degree day because they are scraping the bottom of the laundry barrel. Sometimes natural consequences are the best teacher.)

Clothes Management

With six kids, three of each gender, I have an overabundance of hand-me-downs.

I've slowly learned that paring down clothes is essential. Kids don't need twenty different T-shirts. Having less does mean doing laundry more often, but in the long run it is less laundry, and less clutter. You can Google or search Pinterest for "capsule wardrobe for kids" or "minimalist wardrobe for kids" to find guidelines and even checklists for how many clothing items are really needed per child.

Talk to other moms and find out their strategies. If you have several local friends, you might form a co-op of sorts, where you go to each other's houses on rotating weekends and help out with decluttering and organizing while the kids play together (and then go out for drinks and dinner afterward, while the husbands stay with the kids!).

Whatever you decide, or whatever strategy you employ, remember to give yourself grace and aim for progress, not perfection!

Chapter 7

Pregnancy, Maternity Leave, and Returning to Work

Disclaimer: *In this chapter, the cited laws and regulations are only applicable to mothers who reside in the United States and U.S. territories. If you live outside of the United States, your local laws and policies regarding pregnancy discrimination, parental leave, etc. may differ.*

Pregnancy

Congratulations, you're pregnant! Maybe this is your first child; maybe this is your fifth (or sixth, or seventh …). Either way, a new child within you is cause for joy and celebration. However, growing new life is also a big job, and sometimes balancing the demands of your job with the demands of pregnancy can be a tricky proposition.

It's important to know your rights as a pregnant woman in the workplace. These rights are covered under the Pregnancy

Discrimination Act, which was enacted in 1978 as an amendment to Title VII of the Civil Rights Act of 1964.[19]

In a nutshell, neither your employer nor your boss or supervisor can discriminate against you because you are pregnant. It is illegal to fire you, demote you, dock your pay or benefits, or take any other retaliatory action against you due to your pregnancy or maternity leave. It also means that a prospective employer cannot refuse to hire you because you are pregnant.

If you think any discriminatory or retaliatory actions have been taken against you due to your pregnancy, it is best to consult with a good employment lawyer as well as the United States Equal Employment Opportunity Commission.

Hopefully, you will never face this type of discrimination; but sadly, it still happens in many workplaces. Proving that discrimination has occurred due to pregnancy can often be difficult, so document as much as possible and gather as much evidence as you can in the form of emails, memos, etc.

If you have a verbal conversation with a boss or supervisor or human resources representative that includes possible pregnancy discrimination, recap the conversation in an email and send it to the relevant parties for confirmation. For example: "Just to make sure I understand our previous conversation in Mr. X's office at [time] on [date]: you told me that I would not be receiving a promotion to supervising manager because of my pregnancy. Is that accurate?" Even if they refuse to respond, you at least have documented the time, date, and contents of the negative interaction. The more you have documented, the better — and be sure to back up your documentation to the cloud or a thumb drive, just in case.

Telling Your Boss

It can be nerve-wracking to tell your boss or immediate supervisor that you're expecting — especially if you sense your boss will not react well; if the timing is unfortunate for certain projects; or if you became pregnant before, during, or shortly after the hiring process.

When to tell your boss is entirely up to you. Some women prefer to share the news right away; others prefer to wait until six, twelve, or even twenty weeks. In my opinion, sooner is better, especially if you're dealing with pregnancy-related nausea or vomiting that may require you to request accommodations; however, you can also say that you have a medical condition without elaborating further until you are comfortable doing so.

Regardless of the circumstances, frame your news in a positive matter. Instead of, "I have something I need to tell you," or "I have some news you may not like to hear," say, "I have some happy news that I'm excited to share with you! I'm pregnant!" Hopefully your boss will take his or her cue from you and also respond positively.

Even if you are dealing with less-than-ideal timing — for example, you're a CPA, and the baby is due right in the middle of tax season — do not apologize for being pregnant (and don't feel compelled to share whether the baby was planned or unplanned). Acknowledge that the timing is inconvenient, and pledge to do whatever you can to help with the transition.

If you're dealing with a boss who might respond negatively, remember that you do not have to take abuse. If your boss starts making negative comments or raises his or her voice, say calmly, "I'm not willing to be insulted or yelled at. I'll speak to you about this later, when you're not upset," and walk out (and start job hunting if you haven't already).

Dealing with Rude Comments

In general, I've found there are three ways to deal with negative comments about family size or planning in a workplace context: Defuse with humor, redirect without engaging, or escalate to human resources or management.

1. Defuse with humor. I have an arsenal of humorous responses for every conceivable comment (I think I've heard them all) that may come my way in the workplace (and elsewhere). For example:

> Q: "Don't you know what causes that?"
> A: "Yes, and we're really good at it!"

Make sure that you have a big smile to go with each comment. The less ruffled you are, the more foolish your interrogator will (hopefully) feel.

2. Redirect without engaging. This strategy is helpful if you're receiving comments from someone with whom you need to maintain a strictly professional relationship that isn't conducive to casual joking — clients, customers, upper management, or even coworkers on your team with whom you prefer not to socialize but can't completely ignore. In this case, acknowledge the comment and change the subject, sending a subtle yet definitive message that the topic isn't grounds for discussion. For example:

> Coworker X: "Good gravy, five kids?! Are you crazy?"
> You: "Mmhmm. Say, did you get the memo about the
> TPS reports?"

> Customer Y: "You're pregnant AGAIN? Haven't you
> ever heard of birth control?"
> You: "Yes. Let me know if there's anything else you
> need."

Walk away. Or, if you can't walk away because you're stuck on the phone or behind a counter:

You: "Yes. Is there anything else I can help you with?" or "Yes. Let's take a look at the red Swingline staplers, they might be more to your liking."

VP Lumbergh: "If you could let me know if you're going to have more kids after this one, that'd be great."

You: [bland smile] "We'll see. By the way, when I was working on Saturday I found a glitch in the accounting software … "

Keep acknowledging with short, one- or two-word answers and change the subject. Usually, all but the chronically tactless will get the hint and drop it.

If you happen to be stuck in a workplace with colleagues who can't resist making comments, all you can really do is state your point clearly and firmly. "That's personal; I'd rather not discuss it. Let's talk about Client Project Alpha." Or, "I'd really rather not discuss my family planning choices at work. Do you know the status of the deliverables for Project Omega?"

3. Escalate to HR or management. This solution is a last resort and should be rare (in theory), but it is a viable one if you're constantly bombarded by inappropriate comments or if one specific coworker seems fixated on your situation to the point of giving you constant grief about your family size or pregnancy status. The EEOC specifically mentions pregnancy in its fact sheet regarding workplace harassment.[20]

The EEOC also specifies what workplace harassment is not: "Petty slights, annoyances, and isolated incidents (unless extremely serious) will not rise to the level of illegality. To be unlawful, the

> "My first pregnancy, I was fortunate enough that the hardest part of my first trimester fell during a period between being laid off from one job and starting a new part-time position. God worked that one out really well! This time [is] more challenging, though. Thankfully, I have a wonderful boss and coworkers. I still dread vomiting in the company restroom, though, especially if someone comes in and asks about it."
>
> — Mandy B.

conduct must create a work environment that would be intimidating, hostile, or offensive to reasonable people."

Even if the negative comments you receive don't rise to the level of workplace harassment, you can take action. The first step is to tell your interrogator, politely but firmly, that your family size isn't up for discussion. "Milton, I'd rather not discuss my family planning choices with you. Please don't bring it up again."

If it persists, you can go to your manager or HR. Stick with the facts: "I've asked Milton repeatedly to stop commenting on my family size, but I'm afraid his comments persist. He's brought up the topic five times in the last three days. It's making me very uncomfortable; and as a result, I'm having trouble focusing on my work when he's around. Do you have any suggestions on how to deal with this?"

Any manager or HR rep worth their salt will have a chat with Milton and tell him to cut it out or face consequences (and then enforce said consequences if Milton fails to comply).

Sadly, not all managers or HR reps know how to deal with this type of harassment, and some will try to downplay it or brush it off. In the worst-case scenario, you might have grounds for an EEOC complaint if the harassment becomes pervasive enough.

Pregnancy Nausea while Working

I've had terrible pregnancy nausea during the first trimester (and into the second trimester) of all of my pregnancies. I've had to leave work to go to the emergency room for IV meds and fluids, and I've vomited in more than one workplace toilet. It's made working during the first few months of pregnancy a challenge, to say the least.

I'm a big proponent of better living through chemistry. About two minutes after getting a positive pregnancy test, I call my doctor and ask for anti-nausea medication. I've used phenergan, ondansetron (brand name: Zofran) and Diclegis. Zofran worked the best, but after one of my children was born with a congenital birth defect, I switched to Diclegis out of an overabundance of caution. Talk to your doctor to see what they recommend.

If it's possible to work at home occasionally or more often (even full time) during the first trimester, that can be a big help. It's easier to control your access to a bathroom, and you won't be as mortified if you can't make it and have to use a trash can instead.

Other tricks which have worked for me at various times include:

- Peppermint essential oil (I put it on a cotton ball and sniff when needed)
- Lemon drops or other sour candy
- Ginger Altoids
- Popsicles
- Saltine crackers
- Ginger ale
- Ice-cold Gatorade
- Magnesium supplements
- Preggie Pops (suckers made especially for pregnancy

nausea)

- Candied ginger
- Lemon and ginger herbal tea

Also, I've never been able to tolerate hot coffee in the first trimester, but iced coffee was palatable. Cold soda (even in the mornings!) also helped if I needed a hit of caffeine.

Note: If you have hyperemesis gravidarum (HG) — extreme, persistent nausea and vomiting, to the point where you are losing weight rapidly and can't keep any food or liquids down — you may want to consider requesting medical accommodations and utilizing the Family and Medical Leave Act or short-term disability. HG likely will not respond to any of the suggestions given above and requires more intensive medical intervention.

Business Maternity Wear

Finding attractive, stylish, and affordable workwear is hard enough when you're *not* pregnant, let alone when you are. You don't want to make a large financial investment, because you'll only wear these clothes for approximately six months; on the other hand, quality is expensive, and you don't want to show up to work looking like you made your own maternity dress out of the drapes in your bedroom. Here are some strategies I've found helpful when it comes to business maternity wear:

- Ask relatives and friends if they have maternity clothes they're willing to lend or sell to you, especially if you have coworkers around your size who have been pregnant previously. As an added bonus, whatever clothes they have are more likely to adhere to the dress code. You can also post in local buy/sell/trade Facebook groups.

- You often can find great deals on maternity clothes at department stores if you shop the clearance racks. Discount stores such as Ross and TJ Maxx often have maternity sections too.

- It's hit or miss, but I've found some good pieces at thrift stores and consignment shops. I have had occasional success with online secondhand stores such as eBay and thredUP as well.

- Maxi dresses are a good addition to any maternity wardrobe, if your dress code allows, and can be dressed up with a cardigan and jewelry. As an added bonus, they're very comfortable after pregnancy and are usually nursing-friendly as well.

Coping with Miscarriage at Work

Having a miscarriage is awful in and of itself, but working can add an extra layer of difficulty. Pregnancy can be tricky to deal with in the workplace, even if you're in a supportive environment, and navigating a miscarriage can be a thousand times worse (especially if you didn't want anyone, including your boss, to know that you were pregnant just yet).

Sadly, I have lost four babies to miscarriage, all while I was working full time outside the home, so I have experience in this regard.

If you're in an unsupportive environment, you don't have to tell your boss that you were pregnant or that you're miscarrying or have miscarried; you can simply say that you are undergoing health problems. You can also let HR know if needed. However, I do recommend telling both your immediate supervisor and HR the nature of your health issues. It's easier to explain your exact needs, and it will also help your boss understand that while your physical healing may only take a short while, your emotional healing will likely take longer.

Similarly, I recommend telling your coworkers the nature of your health issues, at least those you work with most closely; I've found that coworkers may be less resentful and more willing to help pick up some slack if they understand why you've had to suddenly take time off, as well as why you may have trouble concentrating once you do return to work. It may also help stifle any nosy questions about when you and your husband plan to have kids (or have more kids).

If you're in a client-facing situation, that's a bit trickier. If your clients already knew you were pregnant, then a brief email is likely the easiest way to let them know. If not, it's probably best just to let them know you'll be out of the office or working a modified schedule due to sudden health issues.

If you've been struggling with infertility, you may want to consider being honest about it with your boss and coworkers. You don't have to go into any great detail, but a simple, "We're dealing with infertility," when asked about plans for children can make people reconsider those personal questions. I've never had to bear that particular cross, but I have had coworkers in that situation, and their honesty with others helped prevent some (but not all) nosy questions.

Take off as much time as you can. I can't emphasize this enough. You are grieving the loss of a child, even if our society doesn't recognize it that way. If your company has bereavement leave policies, inquire about using that leave in lieu of paid time off. If you have available paid time off, take as much time as you can afford. If your loss is later in pregnancy, or if you experience complications, you should also investigate FMLA or short-term disability leave, if offered. Sometimes working can help as a distraction, but if you don't give yourself adequate time and space to grieve your loss, as well as recover physically, it can just get worse in the long run.

Maternity Leave

It's important to find out what your job offers in the way of maternity or parental leave, even if you don't intend to use it soon (or ever). Some employers offer paid or partially paid leave; some offer unpaid leave; some offer short-term disability insurance policies that will cover some or all of your leave; and some have generous PTO policies that will allow you to accrue time to use during your leave.

It's also important to investigate your employer's policies for benefit retention during medical leave. Many employers require their employees to pay some or all of their insurance premiums while on medical leave, so that may be an extra cost to factor into your budget.

Paid Leave

In 2016, 14 percent of civilian workers had access to paid family leave, according to the National Compensation Survey, conducted annually by the U.S. Bureau of Labor Statistics.[21] According to Bloomberg.com: "More than one in three U.S. employers offers paid maternity leave beyond the amount required by law, up from one in six earlier this decade."[22]

The twenty largest employers in the United States, including companies such as Amazon, IBM, and Starbucks, offer various lengths of paid leave; and as of this writing in 2019, four states — California, New Jersey, New York, and Rhode Island — have laws that mandate certain employers offer paid maternity leave to their employees. Washington, DC, and the state of Washington have enacted paid family leave policies as well, but they will not go into effect until 2020.

Some employers' paid-leave policies are contingent upon qualifiers; for example, they only provide leave to employees who have been with them at least a year or who have worked a certain number of hours. These conditions may be negotiable, though, so discuss your options with your employer if you are pregnant but don't qualify for paid leave.

Have your husband check his employer's policies on parental leave as well. More and more employers are instituting parental leave policies that apply to both parents. If your husband qualifies for significant paid leave (say, six or more weeks), you could "switch off" leave times, and have him take six weeks of leave after your paid leave is up. This can help save on daycare costs as well as give Dad a chance for significant one-on-one bonding time with the new baby.

Unpaid Leave

Family and Medical Leave Act
Per the U.S. Department of Labor, eligible employers are required to provide twelve weeks of unpaid leave to eligible employees.[23] (Check with the DOL to see whether you and your employer qualify.)

Your employer may require you to take any accrued vacation time and/or sick time concurrently with FMLA leave, or you may choose to do so yourself. Check your employer's policies to see what they require.

Typically, in order to request FMLA leave, you submit a request to your company's HR department. You'll want to get the ball rolling once you enter your third trimester; FMLA regulations stipulate that you must give your employer at least thirty days' notice if the leave is foreseeable, which maternity leave usually is. However, if the baby comes much earlier than anticipated (or you unexpectedly adopt), you are required to submit your FMLA request "as soon as practicable."

Usually your employer has forms for you to fill out, and forms to give to your doctor to fill out, both of which you return to your employer. Many physicians' offices charge a fee to fill out paperwork and take several business days to complete it. I usually make a mental note to bring my FMLA paperwork when I take my gestational diabetes test at twenty-eight weeks, as I'll be hanging out in the waiting room for an hour anyway; dealing with the paperwork is one way to fill the time.

Bear in mind that you can take FMLA leave intermittently. For example, if you only take eight weeks of FMLA leave and then return to work, you have four additional weeks that you can take in smaller increments. This can be helpful if your new baby has a medical need that requires extra doctor appointments, for example.

My fifth child was born with a birth defect and required regular doctor appointments at a local children's hospital during his first year of life. When I returned to work after my eight-week maternity leave, I requested intermittent

> "My midsize company (fewer than two hundred employees) gives primary caregivers sixteen weeks' paid parental leave. I think the 100 percent mother retention (over the past five years I've been there) speaks for itself. As we plan and push for a more family-friendly workplace, let's pray that God will give us courage and winsome words, and that he will open the eyes and hearts of the decision-makers at our firms to the benefits (for everyone!) of pro-family policies."
> — Abigail C.

FMLA leave in order to take time off for his doctor's appointments. This safeguarded my job, as it guaranteed that my employer could not penalize me for taking extra unpaid time off (I had exhausted my PTO bank during my maternity leave) in order to take my son to his appointments. My husband also applied for intermittent FMLA leave just in case it was needed.

If your employer is too small to be subject to FMLA, or you are not an employee who is eligible for FMLA leave, you may still have unpaid leave. This leave would not carry the same protections as FMLA leave, however: Your employer does not have to hold your job for you, or return you to the same or an equivalent position at the same rate of pay, nor is your employer required to continue your health insurance benefits as they are under FMLA.

If your employer does not have a formal maternity leave policy, you'll need to work that out with HR, your boss, and/or whoever handles benefits. Start this conversation soon after you announce your pregnancy. How much time off you receive depends entirely on your employer's policies. Make sure you get written documentation regarding your arrangement, and keep a copy at home or in the cloud.

Start putting money in savings and/or otherwise preparing to live on one income for the duration of your leave. If you don't already have a budget, this would be a good time to formulate one. Be sure to factor in the cost of any work-related insurance premiums you may be responsible for paying while you are on leave. Also conserve as much PTO as you can during your pregnancy to use during your leave, to minimize the number of unpaid days.

Short-Term Disability Insurance

Some employers offer short-term disability insurance as an employee benefit, usually with the employer paying some or even all of the premium. It's also possible to take out a private short-term disability insurance policy. A short-term disability policy will provide you with a portion (usually 30 to 60 percent) of your pay, starting a week after the qualifying event, in case a medical condition causes temporary but total disability that causes you to miss work for an extended period of time. Recovery from childbirth is included in most policies. Short-term disability leave runs concurrently with FMLA leave and does not provide any sort of job or salary protection. It usually offers only six weeks of paid leave for a vaginal birth and eight weeks for a C-section birth.

Important: If you are already pregnant or become pregnant shortly after you purchase a short-term disability policy or become eligible for one through your employer, you will not be able to file a claim for your upcoming maternity leave. Your pregnancy will be considered a preexisting condition; few, if any, short-term disability policies will cover a pregnancy disability claim that occurs within twelve months of the policy's starting date.

As with FMLA leave, get the ball rolling on a short-term disability claim early in the third trimester. You'll need to provide your short-term disability insurance provider with paperwork very similar to that for FMLA, including a doctor's note attesting to your upcoming disability leave. Once you give birth, you need to call your short-term disability insurance provider as soon as practicable to submit your claim. The exact timeframe depends on the rules unique to your policy.

Working During Leave

Before you go on maternity leave, check to see whether your employer has any policies about work during medical leave. Some employers have policies that stipulate an employee is not expected to and should not perform work during leave.

If you qualify for FMLA leave, your employer is not permitted to interfere with your leave — even if you are taking paid leave — by asking you or requiring you to work. In general, they can contact you with quick inquiries pertaining to the location of documents, with information about salary or benefits, or with other inquiries that can be answered quickly and concisely. However, if they ask you to run reports, or complete payroll, or generate sales leads, those activities would constitute impermissible interference with your leave.

You may be tempted to work during your leave — even if it's only to check emails — but I strongly advise against it. You don't want to get your employer in legal trouble. They are still required to pay you for the work that you do even if they haven't authorized it. Doing a quick scan of your email to set up an out-of-office reply or forward anything pressing usually won't be an issue, as long as it's only a few minutes and the tasks are routine; but if you spend a couple of hours writing emails to clients or working on a project, that is more problematic.

On a more emotional level, the work will keep ... but your baby will not. Even if you love your job and are heavily invested in the work that you do, put the work away and concentrate on your baby. The newborn period goes so fast, and you'll never get those days back. Your boss and coworkers will survive. I promise!

Returning to Work

The Practical

If you are on FMLA leave and/or receiving short-term disability payments, your employer will require your doctor to authorize your return to work. Most doctors can provide the authorization after your six-week postpartum checkup, although some may require another follow-up visit (especially if you had complications and/or a C-section delivery). If your leave is longer than six to eight weeks, you'll want to visit your doctor a week or two before your leave is up in order to secure this documentation for your employer.

Contact your employer approximately two weeks prior to the end of your leave to arrange your return date and time. If you plan to pump breast milk, and you aren't sure whether there is a space available for you to do so, inquire about it at that time.

If you have any flexibility at all with your return date or your daily schedule, arrange to return on a Thursday or Friday, and/or to work halfdays for a week or two. It's gentler on mother and baby to ease back slowly into working after a long leave, especially for a first-time mother. But you may want to take your baby to daycare starting on Monday of that week, if possible, in order to practice your routine and gauge how long it will take to get both of you ready in the mornings.

Prep and pack as much as you can during the evening before so you're not rushing around in the morning trying to get out the door. Enlist your husband, friends, and/or relatives to help out with housework or childcare or meal prep every evening that first week, so that you can spend your evenings snuggling the baby. It's going to be a difficult transition no matter how much you love your job. (Be prepared for reverse cycling — your baby will likely nurse more at night in order to make up for being away from Mom all day.)

Pumping at Work

Once you return to work, you may want to continue providing breast milk for your baby. The rights of nursing mothers have advanced significantly in the last few years, and there are federal laws as well as state laws protecting nursing mothers who choose to express milk for their infants.

KellyMom.com has a great fact sheet regarding the rights of breast feeding mothers in the workplace.[24] Bear in mind that federal law only provides protections for pumping mothers who are nonexempt employees. There is legislation pending that would extend these rights to exempt employees as well; but as of this writing in 2019, that legislation has not been passed. Your state may have laws that protect exempt employees, so be sure to check into those.

If you are a nonexempt employee, your employer is required to give you break time (paid or unpaid) to express your milk, and to provide a private, sanitary place for you to pump that is not a bathroom.

I recommend beginning to pump when baby is four to six weeks old in order to start building up a stash. It's also good to practice setting up and disassembling your pumping equipment. In addition to your pump, breast milk bags, and cooler bags, consider other supplies that are handy for workplace pumping: a hands-free pumping bra, microwave sterilizer bags, gallon-size plastic bags for wet pump parts, cleaning wipes specifically for breast pumps, an

> *"[Returning to work after maternity leave] is really a day-at-a-time thing. It helped me to talk to other colleagues who had to transition back, too. Make sure your weekends once you return are not full of extra stuff so you can just be with your little one and have together time. Be gentle on yourself ... there's so much to balance. It made it easier for me ... to realize that my kids were fine, and it was me who was struggling with the transition."*
>
> — Rita B.

outfit your baby has worn for you to smell (to help with let down and stimulate milk production), and snacks that stimulate milk production, such as oatmeal bars or lactation cookies (check the internet for recipes).

Also, if possible, keep spare pump parts at work. Check with your insurance company; sometimes they will pay for an extra set of parts as well as your pump and the parts that come with it. This will save you from the sickening feeling of arriving at work and realizing that your flanges are still sitting by your kitchen sink where you put them to dry the night before.

The best resource you'll find for working mom pumping hacks is other moms, so join a breast feeding support group (either online or locally) for more tips and tricks!

The Emotional

As I said above, going back to work is always a difficult transition for both mother and baby. I've done it six times, and it's never gotten any easier. You are going to cry, so prepare yourself with tissues and (if applicable) waterproof mascara. The first week is always the worst, but once you settle into a routine it does get easier.

One of the members of the CWM group wrote the following letter to moms going back to work, and I think it is a beautiful expression of the conflicting emotions inherent in that transition:

Dear New Mom Going Back to Work:

I remember vividly the day I went back to work after maternity leave for my first one. I was crying like a baby in the Parisian Metro; my husband was holding my sweet four-month-old, who was my whole world. Then an older woman came to me with a very gentle smile, and she said: "Everything will be okay. YOU will be okay."

As new moms, we're often overwhelmed by a roller coaster of emotions just before going back to work full time: fear, anticipation, sadness, joy, anger! We worry that our child will lose his or her close bond with us, or that maybe we're neglecting the baby by returning to work. Are these feelings normal?

Yes, our feelings are 100 percent valid! But more than that, as a mom of four I can now testify that mom guilt WAS indeed useful to me. It helped me to stay 100 percent focused on my children when I got back home each night, and it helped me tremendously to prioritize my tasks during the day so I could come home and be completely present for them.

The transition is tough, though. So this is the piece of wisdom I want to share with you: Find your tribe, build a strong support team around you — your husband, your close family, a neighbor, a friend! You'll need all the support you can get for this life-changing transition as a new and working mom.

Again, devote your evenings that first week entirely to baby snuggles. It will do both of you a world of good.

What If You Decide Not to Go Back?
During pregnancy, or perhaps during your leave, you may decide to transition out of the workforce, either temporarily or permanently.

This is a complicated decision and one fraught with conflicting emotions.

If you know during pregnancy that you do not plan to return, that is the best time to notify your employer. That way they have ample time to plan for the transition, and perhaps you can even assist in training your replacement before you leave. However, this may cause an issue when it comes to medical benefits, so be sure to factor that aspect into your plans. Your employer may be willing to allow you to keep your health insurance for a month or two after your employment ends as long as you pay the premiums, or your share of the premiums. Another option is to pay for COBRA continuation coverage to extend your benefits; however, that can be very expensive.

If you make the decision not to return to work during your maternity leave, it's best to let your employer know your plans as soon as possible. Again, this may put you in a sticky situation with medical benefits or short-term disability insurance, but your employer will not appreciate being blindsided by the news the day before or even the day of your anticipated return. You don't want to burn any bridges, even if you plan to be a stay-at-home parent indefinitely. Circumstances can change, and you may need your former employer to serve as a reference or help with networking opportunities down the road. They likely will not be willing to give you a good reference if you left them in the lurch at the end of your leave.

What if the end of your leave is approaching, and you are struggling with the idea of returning to work? Try going back to work for a few weeks or a month and see how it goes. You could also commit to live only on your husband's income for your first month or two back at work (less your working expenses). But above all, pray, pray, and pray some more, and keep asking God to show you his will.

Chapter 8
Choosing Childcare

Finding high-quality yet affordable childcare can be one of the most stressful situations that working parents face. We've all heard horror stories about abusive daycare providers and neglectful nannies, and while we'd all love to find and hire Mary Poppins, it seems that British nannies drifting down from the sky aren't too plentiful.

What type of childcare arrangement you choose depends on your particular circumstances and your budget. Today there are a variety of options: daycare centers, in-home daycares, nannies, au pairs, family members, or working opposite shifts. There are pros and cons to each arrangement, and it's up to you and your husband, if applicable, to weigh each option carefully and determine what will work best for your family's needs.

Daycare Centers

A daycare center is a business operation in which many children (typically thirteen or more) are provided care by a team of individuals, overseen by a director, in a freestanding facility that is not the private residence of the director or any of the caregivers.

Advantages

Daycare centers are licensed and regulated by state agencies and must maintain a specific provider-to-child ratio as required by law, as well as adhere to regulations regarding cleanliness and nutrition. They rarely, if ever, need to close due to provider illness or vacation. Their employees typically have degrees or extensive experience in early childhood education. Many centers employ nanny-cams or similar to allow parents to remotely view the facility.

Disadvantages

Daycare centers are usually more expensive than in-home daycare, and not much cheaper than hiring a nanny. There can be extensive waiting lists depending on the location and popularity of the facility. They typically charge exorbitant late fees — for example, $10 per minute — which can be a problem if you run into traffic or get held up at work. You may be required to pay even for days your child does not attend due to holidays or illness. There's less one-on-one interaction between child and provider, as class sizes tend to run large. Due to state regulations, they cannot be flexible when it comes to issues such as illness or immunizations. Children may get sick more often due to being exposed to a greater number of other kids. There can be high turnover of staff, making it difficult for children to form bonds or attachments with their caregivers.

In-Home Daycares

An in-home daycare is a childcare facility in the private residence of the primary caregiver, in which multiple children (anywhere from one to twelve, depending on applicable laws and regulations) are cared for by the sole proprietor or the proprietor along with one or two assistants or partners.

Advantages

In-home daycares are typically the least expensive nonfamily childcare option. Many are licensed by the state or city. There is usually a higher provider-to-child ratio than you would find in a center. They can be more flexible when it comes to scheduling and early or late pickups or drop-offs (although this can vary depending on provider). They can also be more flexible when it comes to illness. For example, they won't necessarily require you to keep your child out of daycare for twenty-four hours every time she runs a fever if they know she is teething, as a center might. The environment is often more "homey," relaxing, and low-key than a center. There's greater opportunity for sibling interaction or interaction with children of different age groups. The same caregiver is always present, making it easier for the child to bond with them.

Disadvantages

Not all states have licensing requirements or regulations for in-home, meaning that in-home daycare providers may not be held accountable to objective state standards when it comes to cleanliness, nutrition, and so on. You need to rely on your own judgment regarding the suitability of the environment for your child or children. They may close, sometimes unexpectedly, due to provider illness or vacations. As with a center, you may be required to pay even on days your child does not attend due to holidays or illness.

Nanny

A nanny is an individual employed by a family in their residence for the purpose of childcare.

Advantages

A nanny comes to your home, so you do not have to deal with pickups or drop-offs at another location. You have complete control over your child's environment and can take appropriate security measures, if necessary. You have one exclusive caregiver for your child or children, which ensures one-on-one care and attention and facilitates bonding. Nannies can, as part of their job, complete household tasks and errands. They will care for your child even if the child is ill. Even though the nanny may have set hours, he or she often can be flexible and acclimate to your schedule, including taking care of your child on specified evenings or weekends.

Disadvantages

Nannies are typically the most expensive childcare option. They are considered household employees, and all applicable tax and employment laws must be followed. Often, it is necessary to offer benefits in addition to salary (i.e., health insurance, paid time off) in order to find and retain a reliable employee. You may be left in the lurch if the nanny unexpectedly calls in sick or abruptly quits. Your child may experience less social interaction with other children. You have less privacy in your home, given that a nonrelated adult will spend most of the day there.

Note: There is also an arrangement known as "nanny-sharing," where two or more families share a nanny and all contribute to her salary and benefits; in return, she cares for all of the children at the location of the families' choosing. This arrangement comes with its own benefits and pitfalls, but some families might be able to make it work, so it is something to consider if you have local friends or relatives also seeking childcare.

Au Pair

An au pair is a young adult, usually between the ages of eighteen and twenty-nine, who travels to another country and stays with a host family for an extended period, usually around a year. Au pairs live with their host families and receive stipends in addition to meals and lodging.

Advantages

Like nannies, au pairs eliminate the need for pickups and drop-offs at another location and will be available even if your children are ill. They are typically treated as family members, facilitating bonding with your child or children. Because they are from another country, they can broaden your child's horizons by exposing them to another culture and language.

Disadvantages

You cannot meet the au pair prior to their placement in your home, and there is the possibility of a bad fit. Au pairs must be provided a private, furnished room with a window, which can be difficult if you have a large family and are already crowded in your home. There is less privacy within the home. Your budget must allow for the increase in utilities and food as well as the stipend for the au pair, which varies according to country (in the United States, an au pair stipend must conform to the minimum wage, meaning the cost is at least $290 per week). They often do not have any formal training or education in childcare. They must be provided with weekends off and two weeks of paid vacation, per the IRS. They may engage in young adult behaviors that you do not approve of. They will leave after one year, meaning your child would need to establish a bond with a new caregiver every year.

"We've done the childcare scramble twice now. Both times, we hired a nanny. First as a long-term nanny-share arrangement. Second as a temporary arrangement until we got a spot at a center. It's ridiculous that the one thing that has made me want to quit my job is childcare frustrations. Not work stress, not wanting to spend more time with my kids, but simply the difficulty in finding quality care for my children at the infant and toddler age. It's such a big gap in the U.S."

— Kristin S.

Family Members

Family members such as siblings, grandparents, or aunts may offer to provide childcare, either in their home or in your home.

Advantages

Often, family members will offer their services for free or at a reduced cost. A family member already has a loving bond with your child, and the environment may already be familiar. Family members will remain in your child's life on a long-term basis. They may be willing to care for your child in your home, either regularly or on occasion. They may be willing to care for your child even if the child is ill. They may have flexibility with their schedules and the ability to start early or work late when needed.

Disadvantages

Given the familial relationship, it may be difficult to establish and maintain clear boundaries. The family member may be disinclined to follow your directives regarding your child's eating, sleeping, etc., in favor of his or her own desires and beliefs. If the relationship sours, either because of or despite the childcare arrangement, you may be obligated to find new (and more expensive) care. Relationships with the family member as well as other family members may be affected if the childcare arrangement causes contention or disagreements. If the family member becomes ill or abruptly decides to terminate the childcare arrangement,

> *"Finding and choosing childcare is one of the hardest things about being a working parent (in my opinion)! With each of my kiddos, I thought, "HOW will we afford this?" and we've been blessed to be able to make it work. I just keep thinking about our huge raise when the kiddos start kindergarten! [It is] definitely a tough decision and process."*
> — Sherri A.

you may be left in the lurch.

Note: Another option for family care is a breadwinner mother and a stay-at-home-father. Obviously, this arrangement only works if the family can manage on one income, but it is worth considering if the mother's earning power exceeds that of the father, and/or the father has expressed interest in taking charge of the childcare and household management.

What About Summer?

If you have school-aged children who aren't old enough to stay home alone, it's always a conundrum to find full-time care during the summer months! There are several possibilities, depending on your area and your budget:

- Day camps, either private or city-sponsored

- Local daycare centers that offer temporary contracts

- A care provider specifically looking for extra income during the summer (maybe a teacher or neighbor)

- A high school or college-age student as a temporary nanny

- Trading work-from-home days with your husband, if circumstances allow

- Sending kids on extended visits to grandparents or other relatives, or inviting a relative to stay with you for the summer.

What Questions Should I Ask a Potential Childcare Provider?

As I expressed in chapter 3, a good childcare provider does not replace your parenting; a provider complements it. You are entrusting this person with your most irreplaceable treasures, and as such you need to be able to have implicit faith and confidence in this caregiver and his or her abilities.

When choosing a childcare location and provider, it's crucial to inspect the former and interview the latter. Always ask for references — and more importantly, CALL the references, as letters can be forged or outdated. I've written letters of recommendation for my childcare providers for them to keep on file, but I've also provided my phone number and email address so that those who want to speak with me personally about my experiences can do so.

Always make sure you get a contract — signed and dated by parents and providers — that stipulates scheduled hours, fees, due dates for payment, accepted methods of payment, late fees, illness policies, sick and/or vacation days, and required notice periods should either of you choose to terminate the contract. It's a good idea to have this in writing even if the provider is a family member.

Search the internet for lists of questions to ask potential providers, as well as lists of red flags to look out for, and print them out or have them handy on your phone so you can take notes.

If the location looks fine and all of the provider's answers sound reasonable, but your instincts are still sending up alarms, go with your gut. A mother's intuition is nothing to sneeze at, and you need to have full confidence in your provider in order to make any arrangement successful.

Childcare is only one part of the equation for a successful working mother. Another part is flexibility, which is essential in order to balance your competing priorities.

Chapter 9
Finding Flexibility

Several years ago, my middle daughter begged to sign up for our city's T-ball league. I felt terrible, because I couldn't figure out how to make it work. The games were mostly on the weekends, but the practices were weeknights at 5:30 p.m. — the exact time I usually arrived home from work. I worked 7:00 a.m. to 4:00 p.m., but I had a ninety-minute commute. My husband worked evenings, and we had no friends or family in the area who would be able to take her to and from practices.

At the time, I was permitted to work from home occasionally, but not as a regular practice. It occurred to me that I might be able to make the T-ball practice schedule happen if I could work from home the same day every week.

I plucked up my courage, went to my boss, and requested permission to work from home Mondays, Wednesdays, and Fridays on a regular basis going forward. I was employing the negotiating tactic of asking for more than I expected to get, so that I could compromise with what I was willing to settle for.

A few days later, I met with my boss again. To my complete and utter surprise, my initial request was granted, and I was given permission to work from home three days per week! Not only was

I able to sign my daughter up for T-ball, but it also made the rest of my life a little easier when it came to scheduling appointments and running errands. As an added bonus, I was able to save on gas and get a little more sleep on those days.

That experience taught me a valuable lesson: It never hurts to ask for more flexibility at work. The worst they can do is say no, and you'll be no worse off than you already were.

The caveat to this, however, is that you often need to earn the privilege of flexibility. If you are on a performance improvement plan or have had negative performance reviews, you are less likely to be granted flexibility, so make sure all of your ducks are in a row performance-wise — unless you can make a really great case for how added flexibility will drastically improve your performance.

What Are My Options?
The flexibility available to you will largely depend on the nature of your work, as well as the individual culture of your workplace.

Switching Jobs
If you work as a teacher or an ER nurse or a manager in a retail environment, working from home isn't going to be feasible in your particular job. In that respect, finding flexibility might mean switching to a new position — such as working from home teaching English to students in China, or working from home for an insurance company's nurse advice line, or even switching industries altogether to a corporate environment. It could also mean switching from a full-time position to a part-time position, either within the same company or with a new employer.

If switching jobs is your only recourse due to the nature of your environment, check out sites such as www.ratracerebellion.com or www.flexjobs.com. Both sites feature companies as well as specific jobs that offer work-from-home opportunities. (Be very wary of jobs on larger job boards that seem too good to be true; for example, offering forty-five dollars an hour for light administrative duties. These jobs are typically scams.)

Some of these positions are full time and offer full benefits, but equally as many are independent contractor positions that do not offer benefits and require you to pay your own state and federal taxes. If you decide to switch to an independent position, it's a good idea to consult a tax professional in order to fully understand the tax ramifications and responsibilities of that particular choice.

Another possibility is a switch to a job in a different setting. If you're a nurse, consider working in a school instead of a hospital; a position as a school nurse, while likely a cut in pay, might offer a schedule that matches the hours your children are in school and allow you to spend school and federal holidays at home with them. If you have a law degree but want fewer hours and more time off than the standard law firm position allows, you may be able to find a position proofreading legal documents or writing articles for legal blogs or journals. Again, you'd likely take a pay cut, but it'd offer more flexibility.

Working from Home

Working from home (also called remote work or telework) is an increasingly common option, especially within the last decade. There are some jobs that are full-time work from home, and others that are based in a physical office but offer the flexibility to work from home, either on set days or on an as-needed basis.

Most full-time telework positions do require employees to have appropriate childcare for their children as a condition of the telework agreement, and for good reason. It's incredibly difficult to divide your attention between needy children and necessary work. It's a bit easier if your children are older and more self-sufficient; but even then, kids have a way of forgetting to respect Mom's work boundaries and run up to pound on her office door if their squabbles get out of hand.

Working from home on an as-needed basis does sometimes mean staying home with a sick child; but again, this arrangement typically only works well if the child is older and can spend the day on the couch watching movies. Of course, there were days when my baby was sick but I had no PTO left, after using it for maternity leave, so I had no choice but to try to work while simultaneously caring for my sick infant. It was not easy, though, and it was an arrangement I chose only as a last resort.

> "What I value most is flexibility, but I have never been in the position of someone [who is] expected to return [to work] days after delivering, or forfeit pay [that] my family needs to survive. I see two main needs: provide better for medically necessary time off, and also provide flexibility: paternal leave, gradual p/t return, permanent p/t return, infants welcome at work, onsite daycare, home office options, flexible work schedule, etc."
> — *Veronica W.*

All this being said, working from home can offer great flexibility, especially if you have a long commute. It adds minutes and sometimes hours to your day that you would otherwise spend in a vehicle or on public transportation. It also allows you to use your lunch breaks or other paid break time to run errands, go to doctor's appointments, get chores done around the house, attend a daytime Mass on a holy day of obligation, or — my personal favorite — take a nap.

If your company doesn't have a telework policy, and you think one is feasible for your position, ask your manager why. It could be that the CEO is convinced that employees who work from home are all slackers who spend their day watching Netflix instead of working; if that's the case, it'll be more of an uphill battle to change that mindset. Or, your manager might be vague, in which case you likely have a stronger argument for teleworking.

If you decide to advocate for teleworking, be sure to highlight how such a program will ultimately benefit the company, as that is what will be most appealing to your boss and those above him or her:

- Employees who are slightly ill — but not too ill to work — can put in a full day, increasing productivity.

- Those same employees will not come to work and spread germs, reducing illness among staff and increasing productivity.

- Added flexibility is a perk for employees, increasing retention and reducing turnover.

- Added flexibility for employees also means increased job satisfaction, which in turn leads to increased productivity.

- A telework program can reduce a company's carbon footprint, which can be a selling point for industry awards or in promotional literature.

There is strength in numbers, so if you're going to pitch a telework proposal to your boss or other supervisors, try to get a group of your coworkers to join you in presenting a viable and well-researched plan.

Most importantly, try to anticipate every potential argument. The strongest objection is usually something along the lines of, "How will we know that employees are working and not goofing off?" (Answer: Implement accountability measures and metrics to determine whether sufficient work is being completed, and revoke telework privileges for those who don't measure up.) Be sure to propose a trial period — say, three months — with a plan to evaluate the arrangement and determine whether the proposed benefits have materialized.

Flexible Work Hours

In environments where teleworking may not be feasible due to business needs or security concerns, varied work hours are a way to provide more flexibility to those who must travel to a physical office each day, or most days. Generally, this means allowing employees to set their own schedules within a particular framework.

For example, many businesses stipulate that employees must be present during specific core hours — such as 10 a.m. and 3 p.m. — but allow employees to choose their own start and end times outside of those hours. So Jane, whose daughter has a 5:30 p.m. ballet class, chooses to work 7 a.m. to 4 p.m.; but John, who really hates rush-hour traffic, opts to work 10 a.m. to 7 p.m. to avoid the worst of it.

Sometimes telework arrangements can be combined with flexible hours. An employee could be permitted to work from home from 7 a.m. to 9 a.m., drive to the office for the core hours of 10 a.m. to 3 p.m., and leave at 4 p.m. This can work well for employees who need to stay at home until children get on the school bus, or who want to avoid morning rush-hour traffic but can't stay late.

Ten-hour work days are another option, permitting employees to work from 7 a.m. to 6 p.m. (ten hours, plus a one-hour lunch break) for four days of the week, and taking off Fridays, Mondays or another day of their choosing. Having a day free to run errands, attend medical appointments, or go out of town for a three-day weekend is often a very appealing alternative to the standard five-day schedule.

Flex time is another arrangement in which an employee can take an hour or two off during the day for a minor emergency or appointment, or to attend Mass on a holy day of obligation, and make up the hours later that evening, or early the next morning, or at some point during the next few days. It's frustrating to have to dip into one's PTO bank just to run a quick errand or leave early to pick up a sick child at school. Flex time makes it easier to deal with life's little bumps without depleting a PTO balance or otherwise suffering a paycheck reduction.

Again, if you're going to pitch flexible working hours to your company, focus on the benefits to your workplace in terms of increased productivity and employee retention.

Bringing Baby to Work

This is a fairly new innovation in the work world, but it has precedent. Some employers, if circumstances and environment are conducive, will allow new mothers to bring their babies to work with them for several months. Obviously, this isn't possible in many positions, for very valid reasons: If you work at a prison or a nuclear power plant, neither environment is particularly conducive or safe for a newborn! But it can be viable in office jobs, especially if the new mother has her own office that's big enough to hold a portable crib or bassinet.

Such a proposal will be a harder sell than teleworking or flexible hours, and there are more complications to consider. Is liability insurance going to cover a child on company property? Will moms be required to sign a liability release? Will the noise or the mere presence of an infant be too distracting for other employees? Will the quality of your work suffer if you have to attend to the baby's needs? How long will the arrangement last? Will it be open to new fathers as well as new mothers?

> "After my third was born, I left a job that I loved and moved into a part-time position making significantly less. While I miss my old job and my coworkers terribly, my family has benefited greatly. The older girls love having more at-home/family time. Money is tight, but I praise God daily that he pushed us to refocus."
> — *Danielle M.*

A lot of these questions can be answered by researching the policies of other companies who have allowed new mothers to bring their infants to work. Remember that it never hurts to ask, and the worst your employer can do is say no — in which case, you're no worse off than you were before.

Job Sharing

Job sharing is when two part-time employees work one dedicated full-time position. This arrangement is not as common as it used to be, but it may be time for a comeback.

Two new mothers at the same company, in the same position, could opt for a job-sharing arrangement. Each would be able to keep her skills current while having more time off and flexibility with her new baby. If one mother has a sick child or is sick herself, or requests a few vacation days, the other employee could fill in for her and work one or two full days until the other is able to return to the regular schedule.

Because they are both dedicated to the same job, no cross-training is needed, and they are both aware of the various details, deadlines, and issues unique to that position. If one employee decides to resign, the other employee can help pick up the slack and contribute to the hiring process — or she could decide to return to the full-time position, eliminating the need for a new hire at all.

An added benefit to the company is that they would still have the work of a full-time employee without paying benefits to a full-time employee (although they can certainly offer benefits to part-time employees, and some do).

Home-Based Businesses

Home-based businesses are another area where flexibility is a significant perk. Many CWM members sell homemade goods on Etsy or work part or full time as freelance writers, virtual assistants, transcriptionists, editors, and so on. It can take years to build such a business to a point where it produces a steady or viable income stream, however, and often you will need to invest money into the business to get it off the ground (meaning it might be a few years before you see any profit). Such businesses might also involve a lot of late nights, early mornings, and weekend work if you're caring for little kids at home during the day.

In-home childcare is one home-based business that can bring in steady and reliable income, supporting other moms who work outside the home. This avenue doesn't offer a lot of flexibility, as you need to be available during your contracted hours, but the benefits include working from home and not having to pay for daycare for your own children. Regulations for in-home childcare providers vary by state, so be sure to investigate your local ordinances and licensing requirements.

A Warning about Network Marketing, Direct Sales, and/or MLMs

Multi-level marketing companies, also called network marketing or direct sales companies, are pervasive in our society. Much multi-level marketing propaganda targets new mothers or reluctantly working mothers. It often promises what sounds too good to be true: staying home with your kids while easily earning a steady income working from your phone only a few minutes per day. The problem is that the data doesn't match the hype.

Per a report done for the Federal Trade Commission by Jon M. Taylor, MBA, PhD, of the Consumer Awareness Institute[25]:

> Of the three-hundred-fifty MLMs I have analyzed for which a complete compensation plan was available, 100 percent of them are recruitment-driven and top-weighted. In other words, the vast majority of commissions paid by MLM companies go to a tiny percentage of TOPPs (top-of-the-pyramid promoters) **at the expense of a revolving door of recruits, 99 percent of whom lose money.** This is after subtracting purchases they must make to qualify

for commissions and advancement in the scheme, to say nothing of minimal operating expenses for conducting an aggressive recruitment campaign — which (based on the compensation plans) is essential to get into the profit column. (emphasis mine)

MLMs make money by selling dreams, not products. While some individuals do succeed financially via their MLM, the vast majority do not. If you are tempted to leave your job because a friend or relative promises that you can "have it all" by working from home, earning a good income, and staying home with your kids, please perform due diligence first. Remember the old adage: If it sounds too good to be true, it probably is.

Chapter 10

Difficult Circumstances

B eing a working mother is not easy under the best of circumstances; but sometimes life gets difficult, and it's hard to see your way through. The problems seem to pile up, one on top of the other, until it seems like there's no way out.

I'm not a marriage counselor, a psychologist, or a medical professional. I can't promise any solutions to your problems. But I can offer you prayers, and the best advice I have as a wife of seventeen years; a mother of six children on earth and four in heaven; and a working woman for over a decade. Whatever your issues, know that you are not alone, and that there are saints in heaven praying for you and your intentions.

Marriage
Disclaimer: My advice below is intended for people in non-abusive situations. If you are in an abusive marriage, or think you might be in an abusive marriage — whether that abuse is physical, sexual, verbal, psychological, financial, and/or cultural — please call the National Domestic Violence Hotline at 1-800-799-7233 (SAFE)

to get advice suited to your particular situation. You can also read about the different forms of abuse in relationships at Reach Beyond Domestic Violence (www.reachma.org), and learn about the Catholic Church's assistance for domestic violence victims in the USCCB document "When I Call for Help: A Pastoral Response to Domestic Violence Against Women."[26]

Marital Problems

Marital problems affect all of us. You can try to "divorce-proof" your marriage, but you cannot "problem-proof" it. When issues do crop up, the most important thing to remember are the vows you took on your wedding day. You and your husband promised to persevere together through all the problems in life. It can be really difficult when it seems like the effort is all one-sided, but your vows remain binding nonetheless. Rest assured that God will provide you grace and peace through all of your tribulations, and he is with you even when you feel abandoned and alone.

Order of Priorities

As Catholics, we have an order of priorities in our lives. These priorities are as follows:

God → Spouse → Children → Family → Friends → Society

For those of us Catholics who are employed, especially for those of us who feel our job is part of our vocation, work fits into this order of priorities somewhere in between family and friends, but within reason. Sometimes our responsibilities at work need to take priority over the desires of our extended family, and sometimes even over the desires (but not needs) of our spouse or children. Sometimes the needs of our spouse or children need to take priority over our work. Careful and continual discernment is the key to deciding where your priorities lie and what needs to take precedence based on your circumstances.

Above all, however, God comes first. This means discerning and following the will of God in our lives, and following all the teachings of his Church to the best of our ability. It means making time for Mass every week, whether or not it is convenient (barring legitimate reasons to miss Mass, such as a child's illness).

It also means making time for prayer every day, making use of the Sacrament of Reconciliation as often as needed, and raising our children in the Faith. As children get older, parents are sometimes tempted to skip Mass when there are extracurricular events on the weekends or while on vacation. However, doing so sets a bad example for children, and teaches them that God is not the first priority in your family.

Second in the order of priorities is your spouse — *not* your children. You and your husband established your family before children came along, and it's your job to ensure that the *foundation* of your family — your marriage — is sturdy and solid. A foundation that has cracks and fissures may crumble under the strain of raising a family, so it is vitally important to build as firm a foundation as possible.

In my experience, this means couples must make it a priority to regularly spend time together — *without children*. This can be difficult to arrange in certain stages of life, but it is a crucial element for building a strong marriage. The surest way to cement the foundation of your life together is to regularly and often spend time together communicating about your family's goals, hopes, and dreams, and remembering why it is that the two of you decided to build a family together.

In some seasons, this might mean slipping downstairs for an hour or two of snuggling on the couch, talking, playing a game, or watching a movie, after the kids are in bed. In other seasons, it means taking a trip away so the two of you can have a few days and nights alone, or scheduling a regular weekly date night. However you manage it, this is the best advice I can give for keeping your marriage strong and healthy.

When Additional Help Is Needed
Sometimes, however, there are problems that run deep and are exacerbated by outside issues — addiction, trauma, or even infidelity. In these cases, reach out to a professional for assistance. Just like we go to a doctor when we are ill, sometimes our marriage needs professional help as well.

Some Catholics are tempted to use their priest as a marriage counselor, but I would actually advise against this unless your priest is a trained and licensed therapist — some are, but not many. Your priest may be a good source for a counseling referral, or if the problem you are dealing with has to do with a theological dispute or similar (for example, a conflict while discerning whether or not to use natural family planning). In most cases, however, you are better off going to a licensed therapist who specializes in marital problems.

To find one, call your local Catholic Charities. You can also search on catholictherapists.com or catholiccounselors.com. Many therapists will conduct sessions over the phone or via Skype, which can be helpful if you're unable to find babysitters for therapy appointments.

If you cannot find a Catholic therapist in your area, or if insurance limits your choices, find a respected and highly rated Protestant or secular therapist who will agree to respect your religious beliefs.

Another resource is your employer's Employee Assistance Program. If your spouse works full time, he might have one too. Many of them offer assistance in finding therapists, and some even pay for the first several therapy sessions.

Do *not* put off marriage counseling or therapy because you are too busy or it's too expensive or it's too much of a hassle to arrange. Your marriage is second only to God in the order of priorities, and everything else — except God — needs to take a backseat while you and your spouse work on the issues you're facing.

If the issues you are facing are not troubling enough for therapy, but still concerning enough that they need to be addressed, work on communication. So many problems are started and/or exacerbated because spouses are talking *at* each other instead of *to* each other, and a lot is being said but nothing is being communicated. Catholic author and therapist Dr. Greg Popcak has authored a book for married couples called *For Better … Forever*[27] that discusses good communication strategies for married couples.

In my experience, when expressing frustration or discontent, it is best to focus on "I" statements, and explain what exactly is at the root of your frustration

"I think every marriage has very difficult stretches. A lot of times, if we don't resolve the underlying resentments and issues, we can go for a good long while without difficulty, but it's kind of right under the surface ready to come out in times of stress. I'm currently in a season where I need to give time and attention to the building up of my marriage to help us through these times of stress. One resource I'm finding useful to cultivate healthier habits is a book called When Divorce Is Not an Option by Dr. Popcak. The title is a little ominous, but I'm finding it to be really useful in learning better habits and managing how I respond to the things I think he needs to work on, since it's really only me I can control."

— Annie A.

while still being respectful to your spouse: "I feel frustrated when I get home and the kitchen is still a mess from supper, because I'm usually very tired, but I feel like I can't go to bed until the kitchen is clean" not "You never clean up the kitchen. Why are you so lazy?"

Adopt a "we" mentality when discussing household issues: "We have a problem with Junior not getting to school on time in the morning. How can we solve this?" instead of, "You keep oversleeping and making Junior late to school!"

Writing a letter or an e-mail to your spouse can help if you're better at articulating your thoughts in writing, but try not to cram too many issues into one document. That can be overwhelming and cause your partner's defenses to go up.

Separation or Divorce

If you are going through this heartbreak, I am so sorry. This is a loss, not unlike a death, so allow yourself to grieve. Set appropriate boundaries with your spouse or former spouse, especially if the marriage is/was abusive or otherwise unhealthy.

If you have a supportive environment at work, confide in your boss so that he or she is aware of the difficulties you're experiencing. Whether or not you confide in your coworkers is up to you, but it might be for the best to forestall any awkward moments, especially if you have talked about your husband in casual conversation before.

It doesn't need to be a big announcement; it's perfectly fine to share it in the context of casual conversations: "By the way, just so you know, John and I are separated and in the process of divorcing" [if applicable]. If you don't want to discuss it further, you can add, "It's a pretty painful topic right now, and I'd rather not talk about it, but I just wanted to let you know what was going on in case it ends up affecting my schedule."

If you don't have a supportive environment at work, it's important to find an outlet to help you deal with the trauma and loss you are experiencing.

Reach out to your church and find out whether it has a ministry for divorced people; some parishes do. If not, DivorcedCatholic

.com is a good resource, faithful to the magisterium, to help divorced Catholics process their circumstances and acclimate to their new situation. There are also Facebook support groups, most of them secret and known by word-of-mouth only. You can also talk to your priest to discern whether filing for an annulment is warranted. Per the United States Conference of Catholic Bishops, "An annulment is a declaration by a Church tribunal (a Catholic church court) that a marriage thought to be valid according to Church law actually fell short of at least one of the essential elements required for a binding union."[28] If your marriage is declared null by a Church tribunal, that would mean you are free to marry again in the Church. Additionally, many who go through the annulment process find it to be very therapeutic and healing, even if they have no intention of remarrying.

In the midst of any marital difficulty, pray, pray, pray. Pray together if you can, and separately if you can't. God knows your frustration, pain, and anger, and he can handle it. Pour out your emotions to him, and rest in his grace and love.

When Natural Family Planning Causes Problems

Using NFP to avoid pregnancy when you have prayerfully discerned that your family circumstances will not allow for another child is not easy (and that's the understatement of the century). It requires a great deal of self-control and self-sacrifice. It can also cause a lot of marital conflict for various reasons. Husbands feel rejected by their wives if they make overtures during fertile periods and are rebuffed. Wives feel rejected by their husbands if they make overtures during infertile times and are rebuffed. Husbands and wives disagree on their reasons for avoiding pregnancy. A non-Catholic or nonpracticing Catholic spouse rejects NFP in favor of contraceptives or sterilization, against the wishes of the other spouse. NFP method or user failures introduce an unplanned pregnancy when life circumstances are difficult because of finances or health issues or fragile mental health.

I love Simcha Fisher's book *The Sinner's Guide to Natural Family Planning*.[29] Chapter 13, "Why NFP Hurts," discusses this issue in depth, and how the small pebbles of misunderstanding and hurt can become large boulders blocking our path to a happy marriage (that's my analogy, not hers).

If you haven't read her book, do so. It's a must-read for all Catholic couples who are using NFP, and she goes deep into all of the marital issues that NFP can cause, offering practical suggestions for dealing with them. Frankly, I think that dioceses should start handing it out at Pre-Cana sessions.

Pregnancy and Children

Children are "the supreme gift of marriage," per the *Catechism of the Catholic Church* (1652), but it's also true that parenthood is not for the faint of heart. We all have had lovely fantasies about our beautiful, healthy, smart, well-mannered children … and then reality sets in. But we discover that reality, even with its quirks, its disappointments, and its obstacles, can actually be better than any fantasy we'd dreamed up. Still, that doesn't discount the difficulties that we can face as we struggle to raise our children in the way they should go.

Special Needs

I have two children with special needs. My oldest has high-functioning autism; my fifth child was born with a congenital birth defect — bilateral clubfoot — and was diagnosed with autism shortly before his fourth birthday. Having a child with special needs is an extra layer of stress on top of the normal hassles of daily life. It's constant second-guessing: Is this the right medication, therapy, or treatment course?

When you're working, the questions increase: Should I be working? Would my child be doing better if I weren't working? How am I going to get my child to and from therapy or treatment while

I'm working? But if I quit my job, how am I going to afford therapy or treatment?

It's a constant tug-of-war, and there are no easy or simple solutions. Best-case scenario? You win the lottery and can afford the best therapies and a full-time assistant to help you coordinate and chauffeur. But for the 99.9999 percent of us who aren't lottery winners ... we do the best we can.

A good support system and an accommodating work environment do help considerably, as does eking out every bit of flexibility you can manage from your job. Take advantage of every local program you can find — public or private — in order to form a local support network of people in similar situations, if nothing else. Online support groups are good too, but local networks have the advantage of helping you evaluate the best therapists, practitioners, care facilities, etc. in your area unique to your child's needs.

If you qualify for FMLA leave, and you haven't used up all of your FMLA allotment during maternity leave, or your FMLA leave has reset, take advantage of the intermittent nature of FMLA leave to protect your job should you need to take extra time off for your child's needs. All it takes is some paperwork for HR and a letter from your child's doctor detailing his or her treatment needs.

Ask for help when you need it, and accept help when it is offered to you. We like to think that we can do it all ourselves, but that's a surefire way to have a nervous breakdown. Most importantly — and I cannot stress this enough — take time for self-care (see chapter 11 for more on this). It's inordinately difficult, especially when your schedule is already crammed with appointments and meetings on top of your regular job, but it's necessary. You can't give of yourself to others if your own reserves are depleted.

Single Parenthood

If you are a single mother, you have my undying admiration. It's hard enough to be a working mother with a husband who is supportive and present; I can't imagine doing it alone. You are amazing.

It goes almost without saying that a single mother needs a support network, but I'm going to say it anyway. Relatives, friends, neighbors, parishioners — find a circle of people who will support you, pray for you, and pitch in to help out when life gets especially crazy.

Find a supportive workplace. This is often easier said than done, especially in a difficult job market, but a boss who will offer flexibility and accommodations is worth his or her weight in gold. If your current job isn't a supportive environment, keep putting out feelers. Workplace stress on top of the stress of single parenting can be a disastrous combo, and your workplace is the only part of that equation that you have the ability to change.

If you are widowed, take as much bereavement leave from work as you can manage. Ask your priest about grief support groups in the area, and don't be afraid to ask for help. There's likely a long list of people who want to help but don't know what, specifically, to do for you. Give them options and accept their help.

Above all, if you're a single mom and feeling overwhelmed, just take things one day at a time. If that's too overwhelming, take things one hour at a time, or even one minute at a time. Break tasks into small chunks. Don't think, "I have to clean the whole kitchen!" Instead, think, "I need to clear off this counter." Then go on to the next counter. Then focus on the dishwasher. Even if you don't get it all done, it's okay — the goal is progress, not perfection.

Give yourself grace, and do the best you can with what you have, focusing on the needs of the present moment.

Health

Physical Health Issues
If you're experiencing physical health issues that affect your abil-

ity to work, investigate the possibility of requesting reasonable accommodations from your employer under the auspices of the Americans with Disabilities Act.[30]

Reasonable accommodations can include a change in schedule or work location, adaptive equipment, extra breaks, and so on, and your employer is required by law to accommodate you unless they can prove that providing the accommodations would cause "undue hardship" (a difficult standard to meet).

If you qualify for FMLA leave, it isn't limited to childbirth or care of a family member; it can also be taken if you have "a serious health condition" that makes you "unable to perform the essential functions of [your] job." Hyperemesis gravidarum during pregnancy is one example of a health condition that would warrant FMLA leave.

If workplace stress is causing physical health problems, the most important thing you can do is speak up. If your workload is too great, talk to your manager about prioritizing the most important tasks, or getting extra help. If your coworkers are in a similar situation, try using the "strength in numbers" approach and going to your manager, or higher on the ladder, as a group.

If your manager is unsympathetic or denies there is a problem, you can either go above his or her head or accept that you're in a toxic workplace and start looking for a new position. You can also resign, but few people are in a position to be able to do so. Regardless, *no job* is worth sacrificing your health. It can be hard if you are in a job where you sincerely believe in the mission, or one that you consider your vocation, but you can't work most effectively toward your mission if your health is suffering. Perhaps God is calling you to work elsewhere, or to take a break to focus on your physical well-being.

Mental Health Issues
Mental illness still carries considerable stigma in our society.

Unfortunately, to many it is still seen as a moral failing or a sign of weak character, instead of a neurochemical imbalance.

If you have a mental illness or think you may be struggling with one, know that you are not alone. It's estimated that one in five people in the United States is affected, according to the National Alliance on Mental Illness.[31]

Trying to balance work on top of mental health issues can be extremely challenging. I have not struggled with mental illness myself, but my husband has Type II Bipolar Disorder, and we often talk about the challenges he's facing — at work and at home — as he manages his illness. I've learned a lot from him, and from friends in similar situations, about strategies at work and at home for those who are having a difficult time.

If you haven't sought medical help, do that first. It is no different than going to the doctor because you have strep throat or bronchitis. With mental illness, there is a chemical imbalance in your brain that warrants treatment. As a popular internet meme about mental illness says, "If you can't make your own neurotransmitters, store-bought is fine."

That being said, medication alone doesn't always solve the problem. Sometimes it takes quite a bit of trial and error before you find the right medication or the right dosage. My husband tried several medications before finally finding one that worked well for him and had manageable side effects. Even now his psychiatrist sometimes tweaks his dosage or adds or changes medication to help with additional problems.

However, getting medical treatment is still the first and best step. If you have an EAP, contact the provider and see what mental health services are offered. Contact your insurance company for help in finding a psychiatrist in your insurance network. It's okay to ask your spouse or a friend to help you do these things, even if he or she just stands next to you for moral support or sends you an email as gentle encouragement.

If your work is suffering due to your struggles, talk to your boss. He or she may be more sympathetic and more willing to work with you knowing that you have a medical problem, and that you are seeking treatment. You can discuss strategies for accountability and task management. You can also request intermittent FMLA leave to ensure your job will be protected if you take time off for appointments or therapy, and you can request reasonable accommodations under the ADA. (Mental illness is considered a disability!)

> "There is nothing to be ashamed of when we struggle with mental illness. I have anxiety and take medication to help me. I also had PPD after each of my children were born, but I had it really bad after my last child was born. I had to pray the Rosary many times during the night, but it helped."
> — *Debbie G.*

A popular advice blog, Captain Awkward, has a marvelous article called "How to Tighten Up Your Game at Work When You're Depressed."[32] It contains practical advice and coping strategies, ones my husband has used often, for managing your work and your mental illness.

The most important point is keeping the lines of communication open, to the point of sending daily emails to your boss summarizing the status of your tasks and projects or having daily check-ins to monitor the progress of your work. If your boss sees that you are making an effort and doing what you can to manage your work, he or she is more likely to give you the time and breathing space you need to make positive changes.

Talk to your family, too, especially your spouse and children. Share your struggles and try to outsource or delegate as many household tasks as you can so that you can focus on your health.

It's okay to take a break when it comes to extracurricular activities or volunteer work.

It will likely be a long road, and it won't be an easy one, but God is walking right beside you.

Finances

My husband and I have been married for seventeen years, and we're just now getting to a point in our marriage where we aren't struggling and living paycheck to paycheck. For years we've been barely scraping by, what with the high cost of daycare, several layoffs, and lots of medical bills.

I am not at all an expert when it comes to finances or dealing with financial troubles, so my advice is going to be very general. It's always best to seek advice from a financial planning professional, or someone who specializes in budget help and debt management.

The first step to solving financial problems is to take a hard look at your financial situation, taking stock of all income and expenditures. Carefully tracking spending for a few weeks or several months will give you the best idea; but in the meantime, you can get a good idea of where your money is going by looking at your bank statements.

There are a million ideas online for frugal living and cutting spending, but none of them will be effective if you and your spouse don't change your attitudes toward spending. Both of you need to be fully committed to changing your spending habits in order to bring about real change.

If there is a gambling or shopping addiction in play, it may be necessary to cut off the addict from any and all access to bank accounts, credit cards, and online accounts. Addicts are very clever and canny at hiding their addiction and finding ways to spend or get gambling money, so it is best to seek help from addiction professionals who can advise you further.

If the problem is particularly bad, or if the addict is unwilling to attend twelve-step meetings or any other form of addiction treatment, separation may be necessary to protect your own finances and the financial future of your children. Again, consult a lawyer if you feel this step needs to be taken.

If you have a very high debt-to-income ratio, your first step is to look at what you can do about the debt. Your options will depend on the type of debt you've incurred. If it's student loan debt, you can sometimes work with lenders to qualify for income-based repayment programs, forbearances, or deferments. If it's medical debt, you can often work with hospitals and doctors' offices to arrange payment plans that will fit your income.

Check your Employee Assistance Program, if one is offered by your employer, to see whether they offer any solutions, such as consultation with a credit counseling company or a debt settlement program. Credit counselors can often give advice and present solutions you may not be aware of, and can also advise you about reliable debt settlement or consolidation programs.

Debt settlement or consolidation companies will attempt to negotiate settlements with your creditors on your behalf. However, be *very* cautious when considering a debt settlement or consolidation program; many are scams. Always thoroughly research the program first, and check into its rating with the Better Business Bureau.

If your debt is significant, you may want to consult a lawyer or other financial professional about bankruptcy proceedings. Chapter 7 bankruptcy involves selling most of your assets (which can, but not always, include your house or car) to pay your creditors. Chapter 13 involves establishing a court-ordered and income-based repayment plan to pay creditors. Both can negatively affect your credit for approximately seven years, so it's more of a "nuclear solution" when you don't have any viable options left.

Of course, there's always the possibility of increasing income by taking on an additional job. My husband drove for Lyft and Uber for several years, on top of his full-time job, in order to make ends meet. I occasionally write freelance articles to bring in income. Working more than one job, while necessary at times, is extremely hard on family life, though, so practice careful discernment before taking this step.

You can also ask your current employer for a pay raise, or find a new job with increased pay, depending on your circumstances. It's worth keeping feelers out, as you never know what may come along.

Chapter 11

Prayer, Fellowship, and Self-Care

Prayer, fellowship, and self-care are three essential tools in the Catholic working mother toolbox! We need prayer to strengthen and maintain our relationship with God; fellowship to support and bond with our sisters in Christ; and self-care to replenish our reserves so we can more readily and ably give of ourselves to others.

However, all three are increasingly difficult to fit into our busy schedules, and all too often a working mother neglects to prioritize one or more. Pope Saint John Paul II once said in a homily, "As the family goes, so goes the nation, and so goes the whole world in which we live."[33]

Similarly, as the mother goes, so goes the family. If the mother is overwhelmed, unhappy, stressed, miserable, and spiritually unfulfilled, the family will suffer accordingly. In other words: "If mama ain't happy, ain't nobody happy!"

But how do you fit prayer, fellowship, and self-care into your schedule when you're already stressed and busy? What follows are some tips and tricks that I and other CWMs use to keep ourselves prayerful, social, and recharged.

Prayer

Finding Time for Prayer

The key to a consistent prayer life is routine. Picking a specific time to pray, or a specific activity during which to pray, really helps form the habit. Once we establish the mental connection between the time or the activity and prayer, it will become almost second nature.

Several Catholic working mothers who are nursing like to use their pumping time at work as their dedicated prayer time. It's usually the perfect amount of time to pray a Rosary or a Divine Mercy chaplet, and the rhythmic *whooshing* sounds of the pump are an oddly fitting accompaniment. Some keep a rosary in their pumping bag for this purpose; others use a rosary app or listen to an audio file or video on their smartphone.

> "Has anyone else figured out this awesome way to pray multiple times while at work each day? I set my computer password to the acronyms of a prayer. Last month was "sjp4u" for "Saint Joseph, pray for us." I had to update it last week, and I'm asking for Our Lady, Queen of Peace, to pray for us ... about twenty times a day."
>
> — Beth M.

I like to use my computer login password to remind me to pray. That way it is a constant reminder over the course of the day. For example, I'll set my password to "H@1L M@ry Full 0f Gr@c3" (note: *not* an actual password of mine); every time I log in, it's a reminder to pray a Hail Mary.

My personal prayer time is in the morning, before I get out of bed. I receive the Blessed Is She daily email devotional (blessedisshe.net), which contains a link to the day's Mass readings and a short devotional, written by a fellow Catholic woman, that relates to that day's readings. I also receive Bishop Barron's Word on Fire Gospel reflection, a daily Bible verse, and a daily excerpt from the writings of C. S. Lewis. They're all waiting in my inbox when I wake up and check my email. I make an effort to read them all in the morning, before I start my day, and to pray and reflect on what I've read.

Occasionally I'll also have an email from Pray More Novenas (praymorenovenas.com), which is a ministry that encourages Catholics to pray novenas together as a worldwide community and offers regularly scheduled novenas for the faithful to pray together. They send an email every day of the novena with that day's prayer, and they also offer audio, video, and podcast links to the novena prayers. Their name is apropos, because I've definitely prayed more novenas since I signed up!

If you're fortunate enough to work near a Catholic church or adoration chapel, or if you work for a Catholic organization, diocese, or parish that has its own church or chapel nearby, there's always the option of dropping by on a paid break or lunch break, or before or after work, for private prayer time or even adoration.

If you have a commute, that provides an ideal time to pray. My most recent commute was exactly thirty-five minutes, and it was the ideal amount of time to pray a Rosary. I got in the habit of praying the Rosary every morning on my way to work, and it really started off my day on a positive note.

You can also pray short prayers while doing monotonous household tasks, such as washing dishes or mopping, and you can pray with your family at mealtimes and before bed. Prayer doesn't have to be a long, drawn-out process or always take place in a quiet location. You can pray inwardly no matter where you are or what you are doing. It can be as simple as a brief "Mary, mother of Jesus, be a mother to me now" (one of the favorite prayers of Saint Teresa of Calcutta!) or "Jesus, I trust in you" before a meeting or when you arrive home.

> "Find a parish with more community life. When I first moved to New Jersey, I shopped parishes till I found one that met my needs at the time. I was a divorced, single mom with a five-year-old and eight-year-old who had just moved to New Jersey and had no friends or family. I sat down and I talked to the priest, and he suggested that I meet up with a girl [whom] he thought I would get along with. This woman is one of my closest friends to this day and godmother to one of my children."
>
> — Mel C.

My husband and I currently split Masses because our five-year-old with autism doesn't do well in church. I go to a morning Mass, usually at 11 a.m., with my two older daughters, and he goes to an evening Mass with our two oldest sons. I will take the opportunity to stay at Mass for ten or fifteen minutes after it ends so I can have some prayer time (before Mass would work too, but I can barely make it on time, let alone early).

Fellowship

Human beings are social creatures, and we are designed to exist in a society, not in isolation. Even the most introverted among us (*raises hand*) crave time spent with trusted friends and loved ones.

Outside of our family circle, we gravitate toward those who are most like ourselves, or with whom we share a strong bond of commonality. As I said in chapter 1, the most repeated refrain I hear after women join the CWM group on Facebook is, "I thought I was the only one! I'm so glad I'm not alone!" or some variation thereof.

Rebecca Frech's latest book, *Can We Be Friends?*, explores this concept thoroughly. It's a discussion of the purpose and importance of friendship; different types of friends; and how to foster and facilitate good friendships.

She writes:

We're not meant to be solitary creatures. Way back in the beginning, God looked at Adam and declared that it wasn't good for man to be alone. It wasn't long before God created Eve. They had a couple kids, and then a few more. Those first people could have spread out and gone anywhere, but history shows us that they mostly stayed together. They congregated in tribes and then towns, not just for safety but also for companionship. Fast-forward thousands of years and we're still congregating, not just in person, but in virtual villages and communities. Still, we're left wondering, How can a society that centers on constantly being connected have so many people feeling as if they are all alone?[34]

While online communities such as CWM are wonderful, they're only part of the equation. Virtual friends are great, but there's something to be said for the in-person connection of "real life" friends too — someone you can meet at your favorite coffee shop for a latte and a chat. Someone you can meet at a park and catch up with while your kids run wild on the playground. Someone you can call when you're home with three of your kids who are sick with the flu; your husband is at work; and you desperately need someone to drop off a pot of chicken soup and a bottle of wine. Someone who offers a shoulder and a sympathetic ear when things aren't going so well at work, or you've suffered a death in your family.

Finding Your Tribe
Finding these friends is the tricky part. We're all so insulated with social media, and so busy driving all over the place for different events and activities, that it's become more awkward and difficult to make those real-life connections.

Coworkers can develop into good friends, but sometimes

navigating those relationships can be tricky, too. I have always made an effort to put clear boundaries between my work life and my personal life. That's not to say I never socialized with my co-workers outside of a work context, but it wasn't typical.

So how can you find your tribe?

The internet can be a useful tool. I've used Facebook to my advantage by joining many Facebook groups for residents of my city and making connections there, including a group specifically for Catholic women in my metro area. Blessed Is She, the group I mentioned above, also has Facebook groups for women in specific regions of the United States (Northwest, Southwest, and so on), and the members of those groups regularly schedule brunches and other gatherings so members can meet up in person and learn more about one another.

I also started an optional Member Location Gallery photo album in the CWM group so individual members could comment on a picture of their state flag and hopefully find other group members who live in their area. Several members have organized local meetups or have started subgroups for Catholic working mothers in their cities or regions.

Events and gatherings at your local parish can be a good way to find in-person friends as well, especially if your parish has a specific ministry for moms. However, in my experience, many of those ministries are geared toward stay-at-home-moms and hold their events on weekdays, so that may not be feasible. It's also difficult to get out to events during the weekend when you are trying to catch up on housework or laundry.

Of course, one of the best ways to find friends is to pray and ask God to lead good friends into your life! Saint John the Apostle is the patron saint of friendship, and I think Saint Gianna would be a good intercessor, too. (She usually is for working moms!)

If and when you do find local friends, it can still be a challenge to see each other, because you're all so busy — especially if you're all working moms! So how do you find the time to get together?

Being Intentional about Gatherings

There's an old adage that says, "People make time for the things that are really important to them." That's especially true for busy working moms. If we're going to do something, it needs to be scheduled, preferably weeks or even months in advance. Spur-of-the-moment gatherings can be fun; but logistically, they are more difficult to organize.

So, be intentional. Talk with your friends and figure out what types of activities you're interested in and can afford. Playdates for the kids? A girl's night out at a local restaurant? Meeting at the local library for a book discussion? Shopping at a local mall or department store? Catching a movie or play at the local theater? A nature hike at a local state park? Zumba classes at the gym? Attending Mass together and going to brunch afterward? Manicures and pedicures?

> *"I find that now [that] my kids are in Catholic school, the doors of friendship with other Catholic practicing moms [are] opening because of involvement in school. I also participated in a Bible study that met in the evenings from 8 p.m. to 10 p.m. It was a great time for a working mom, and I got to meet other working Catholic moms, not just SAHMs."*
>
> *— Jennie D.*

Once you figure it out, pick a date and schedule it. Schedule several if you can. Mark it in your calendars and make a pact not to cancel unless a genuine emergency or serious conflict arises. If you need childcare, tell husbands they are on the hook that night, or beg favors from relatives. Even better, maybe your real-life friends have teenage children who don't mind earning a little extra cash. If finding childcare isn't feasible, you might have to plan some kid-inclusive gatherings for a while.

I've always wanted to organize a cadre of working moms to do marathon decluttering or laundry or housecleaning sessions at each person's home, followed by wine and pizza or even dinner out. Sadly, I don't (yet) have enough local friends to make that happen. But maybe someday …

Being intentional about your gatherings accomplishes two things: (1) it strengthens the bonds of friendship, and (2) it provides an outlet for fellowship, which is integral for introverts and extroverts alike. It can also be an important element of self-care.

Self-Care

Have you read Jennifer Fulwiler's *One Beautiful Dream* yet? If not, you *must*. This book speaks to a Catholic mama's heart.

One of my favorite parts in the book is when she talks about how mothers are constantly called to serve others, but don't or feel they can't take the time to serve *themselves*. They feel like their needs and dreams and passions need to take a backseat to the needs of their family or their job or their spouse. But it's just the opposite: In order to *keep* serving, it's so very crucial that a mother takes time to do what rejuvenates and refreshes her.

Fulwiler appeared on the podcast "Fountains of Carrots," hosted by Haley Stewart and Christy Isinger, on April 30, 2018, shortly before the release of *One Beautiful Dream*, and she explained this concept beautifully.

She began by discussing the secular mentality — one she used to be immersed in as an atheist working in a tech firm — that you don't dedicate your life to having kids or raising a large family; you have one or two kids, you raise them, and then you are "done" with that season of your life. But for Catholics, that season can often last twenty years or more; for us, service isn't a temporary situation — it's a lifelong vocation. She said in the podcast:

Real life, for the Christian, is service, and if you are in this for the long term, you *have* to rejuvenate yourself, you *have* to make room for your passions. You *have* to make room to recharge your batteries, because otherwise you will just burn out, and you simply will not be able to live an entire life dedicated to service.

I realized, this just doesn't feel right, this idea that's out there mainly [in] Catholic and some Christian worlds, the idea that if you are a good Christian mother, you put ALL of your self-care on hold, you put everything on hold when you have little kids. [...] No. This is wrong. This is absolutely wrong.

One of the lines I say in the book [...] if you keep putting your own needs — not just needs, but passions and desires — on hold, you will burn out. And eventually, one of these two things will go [...] basically, eventually, you will stop serving. You can't keep running yourself ragged over decades. You can do it for a couple of years, but you can't do it for decades. And so you'll just stop serving. And so I came to realize that following your passions, demanding that you have time for self-care, is a central part of a life dedicated to service."[35]

Isn't that a great point? "Following your passions, demanding that you have time for self-care, is *a central part of a life dedicated to service.*"

So What Is Self-Care?
Self-care is much more than treating yourself to a slice of chocolate cake after supper or getting a massage occasionally. It's looking at all aspects of your life and determining what activities rejuvenate you instead of taking from you.

Self-care takes different forms. It could be adoration, private prayer, writing, running, going to the gym, getting a massage, going out with friends, having regular time alone in a quiet place to read a book, etc. Every person is different.

Olga Phoenix, MPA, MA, is a trauma professional (someone who works to prevent and treat vicarious trauma, compassion fatigue, and related issues in high-stress careers such as medicine or firefighting). She's also an expert in the area of self-care. She created a self-care wheel[36] to help men and women evaluate their specific self-care needs for each area of their lives. The areas she lists on the wheel are: physical, psychological, emotional, spiritual, personal, and professional. All are distinct needs, although many can overlap.

Physical
Physical self-care is how we treat our bodies. We need regular activity, healthy food, and plenty of sleep. In some seasons of life, this is a tall order! It can also include pampering our bodies to help induce relaxation and reduce stress. My favorite relaxation technique is to take a hot bath with lavender-scented Epsom salts. I have a bathtub caddy that holds a book, a candle, and a glass of wine, and I will sit and soak, reading and sipping and listening to a relaxing playlist. It's heavenly, and I always feel much more relaxed and happier after a bath.

Physical self-care can mean getting regular manicures or massages; blocking out regular time for exercise or participating in a favorite sport; splurging on beauty products or clothing that makes you feel pampered and attractive; having the time to take a walk alone while listening to music or podcasts; or taking time to eat a leisurely meal (or, at the very least, being able to eat a meal while it's still hot).

Psychological
Psychological self-care is having the time and opportunity for reflection and quiet. It can be getting out into nature; journaling; practicing self-kindness; saying no to extracurriculars or requests for volunteer work when you are feeling overwhelmed

or stressed; taking time for intellectual stimulation (going to a museum or a book discussion); or engaging in a hobby or other activity that makes you feel proud of yourself or gives you a deep sense of accomplishment.

My favorite type of psychological self-care is having the opportunity to read. I must read for enjoyment every day in order to feel happy and fulfilled, even if it's just fifteen minutes before I go to bed. I also enjoy having the time to visit the library or a used bookstore.

Emotional

Emotional self-care is caring for your sense of self-worth and your need for affection. It can mean taking time for self-affirmation; cuddling with a loved one or a pet; creating healthy boundaries in your life; asking for help when you are feeling overwhelmed; and cut-

> *"[Self-care] is not mythical; it is something you have to schedule just like anything else or it doesn't happen. It IS something that should happen, on a regular basis, because 'you can't pour from an empty cup,' right? For me, I find I get resentful or throw lots of pity parties for myself if I don't take care of myself. I joined a book club after moving to meet people AND to make sure I got out once a month with people who did not need anything from me. I take a hot bubble bath. (My kids are older so I can actually do this.) I have even sent myself flowers when I felt neglected romantically and unappreciated. It felt GREAT! Even Mother Teresa took time off from time to time."*
> *— Holly R.*

ting yourself slack when you're experiencing difficulty in your life. It can be letting go of the need to have a perfectly clean house and accepting the mess as part of your particular season of life. It can be admitting that you are in survival mode and acting accordingly.

Spiritual

As Catholic women, our spiritual self-care is crucial! We need time, at a minimum, to attend Mass weekly and to take advantage of the Sacrament of Reconciliation as often as needed. We need time to cultivate our prayer life and nourish our spiritual health by reading or listening to devotional materials. Some women find that making time for daily Mass or a weekly adoration hour helps to refresh and rejuvenate them.

I make it a priority to attend my area's annual Catholic women's conference; afterward, I go out to dinner with my friends who also attended — an example of intentional fellowship. I'm always on a "spiritual high" for days and sometimes weeks after the conference, and I look forward to it every year. I've also taken the time and spent the money to go to Catholic spiritual retreats when I have felt the need for a "spiritual pick-me-up."

One of the members of the CWM group attends adoration weekly with her young toddler, "Miss Eva" — and she's done so since before Eva was born. Every week, she posts that she and Miss Eva are heading to adoration and solicits prayer intentions. As it turns out, Miss Eva is quite the powerful intercessor, and we've had many answered prayers as a result, thanks to her and her mama's commitment to their spiritual self-care. Miss Eva's little brother will be born in a few months, and he will accompany his mama and big sister on their trips to adoration. We call them "the prayer babies."

Personal

Personal self-care is caring for our sense of self. It is making time to celebrate who we are and the distinctive characteristics that define us as beloved children of God and unique individuals. This can take the form of making time for or cultivating personal hobbies, such as sewing, handicrafts, writing, blogging, reading, watching a favorite or anticipated movie or television show, cooking, baking, gardening, rock climbing, or a plethora of other activities. It's also meeting with friends, spending quality time with our family, or simply having the chance to sit and write out some short- or long-term personal goals.

Professional
Yes, professional self-care is just as important as the other elements of self-care! It can include making time for lunch; setting healthy boundaries with bosses, coworkers, and direct reports; managing overtime (e.g., not working excessive amounts of overtime on a regular basis, or declining to work overtime if it is interfering with your health or well-being); leaving work at work and not allowing it to interfere with family life (easier said than done with some professions); taking vacation days and/or mental health days when necessary for relaxation and rejuvenation; and taking the time to set and work toward professional goals, including continuing education.

Typically, working moms with very young children don't have an abundance of time off available on a regular basis (it's used up for maternity leave, pregnancy leave, or to care for sick children), but if you are fortunate enough to accrue a decent amount of paid time off, make it a priority to use it!

If possible, occasionally take a vacation without kids, even if it's just an overnight trip or taking the kids to Grandma's house for the night so you and your husband have a quiet evening alone. Your marriage needs care and attention so the two of you can keep building on that strong foundation, and raising happy, thriving Catholic kids.

Epilogue

It is my sincere hope that this book has been an encouragement and an inspiration to my readers!

It's been quite the learning experience writing it, and I hope it is both edifying and useful as you navigate all the hills and valleys of being a faithful Catholic, employee, and mother.

As Catholic working women, we live out our feminine genius at home and in the workplace by showing that women do not have to be confined to the boxes that society likes to put us into (whether that is Catholic society or secular society). We can work *and* have a family, even a large family. Is it easy? No! But nothing worth doing ever is.

Part of our vocation as Catholic working mothers is to help work for a better world so that people will have more choices, instead of being bound by their circumstances. We want a world in which a woman who feels called to stay at home and homeschool her ten kids can do so; a woman who feels called to work full time outside the home and send her three kids to public school can do so; and neither woman will feel she *has* to stay home or she *has* to work.

We need women and mothers in the workplace. We need women who know the particular challenges that working mothers face so we can encourage employers to make changes that benefit women need or even want to work — and that similarly benefit fathers. Working moms have so many skills that are valuable to employers: We're scheduling ninjas, we can work with many different personality types, and we can bring order to chaos, to name a few.

We've still got a long way to go, and it is getting harder to live on one income in our society; but I think that if we as working mothers push for more flexibility in the workplace for all parents, and encourage "working to live" instead of "living to work," we can foster a society that encourages a dynamic of work *and* family, instead of work *versus* family.

If this sounds like an ideal you're eager to work toward, or if you simply want more support in your journey as a Catholic working mother, please feel free to join the Catholic Working Mothers community. You can find our Facebook group, Catholic Working Mothers. You can also follow my Facebook page, Catholic Working Mother or follow my Patheos blog, "The Catholic Working Mother."

Our community is vibrant and robust, with Catholic working mothers from varied walks of life.

Again, remember that you are not alone. This is a crazy life, but it can be a rewarding one, too. Like Saint Gianna Beretta Molla, who "with simplicity and equilibrium [...] harmonized the demands of mother, wife, doctor, and her passion for life," may you also find peace and fulfillment in pursuing your dual vocation as a mother and an employee.

Saint Gianna, *ora pro nobis*!

Appendix 1

Other Tools for Discernment

Helpful Novenas

- Novena to Saint Gianna Beretta Molla
- Novena to Mary, Undoer of Knots
- 54-Day Rosary Novena
- Novena to Saint Joseph the Worker
- Novena to the Holy Spirit
- Novena for Work to Saint Josemaría Escrivá
- Novena to Saint Cajetan, Patron of the Unemployed
- Saint Thérèse of Lisieux Novena (specifically, ask her to send you roses, or a rose in a specific color, as a sign — apparently a lot of people have had success with this method)
- Novena to Sts. Louis and Zelie Martin
- Novena to Saint Teresa Benedicta of the Cross

Readings

If you haven't already, be sure to read Dr. Stacy Trasancos' advice on discernment in chapter 4.

Catholic theologian Dr. Peter Kreeft has an excellent article about discernment on his website: http://www.peterkreeft.com/topics/discernment.htm

Several members of the CWM group recommend "An Ignatian Framework for Making a Decision" (there is even a printable worksheet!) at https://www.ignatianspirituality.com/making-good-decisions/an-approach-to-good-choices/an-ignatian-framework-for-making-a-decision.

Appendix 2

Prayers for Working Mothers

T hese are some of my favorite prayers for mothers that I've found while tooling around the internet. The first is especially dear to my heart.

Reluctant Working Mother's Prayer[37]
O Lord, since I must now entrust my precious child into the arms of another so that I may go forth to earn bread for our table, accept my offering of tears and deep regret.

Take my child, Lord — and my aching heart — and lay them together in your dear mother's lap, where both may rest secure until I come again to claim my treasures.

Amen.

Prayer to Saint Joseph for Success in Work[38]
Glorious Saint Joseph,
model of all those who are devoted to labor,
obtain for me the grace to work conscientiously,

putting the call of duty above my many sins;
to work with thankfulness and joy,
considering it an honor to employ and develop,
by means of labor,
the gifts received from God;
to work with order,
peace, prudence, and patience,
never surrendering to weariness or difficulties;
to work, above all,
with purity of intention,
and with detachment from self,
having always death before my eyes
and the account which I must render of time lost,
of talents wasted,
of good omitted,
of vain complacency in success,
so fatal to the work of God.
All for Jesus,
all for Mary,
all after thy example,
O Patriarch Joseph.
Such shall be my motto in life and death.
Amen.

A Single Parent's Prayer[39]

Lord, grant me:

Time enough ...

to do all the chores, join in the games, help with the lessons, and say the night prayers, and still have a few moments left over for me.

Energy enough ...

to be bread-baker and breadwinner, knee-patcher and

peacemaker, ballplayer and bill juggler.

Hands enough ...

to wipe away the tears, to reach out when I'm needed, to hug and to hold, to tickle and touch.

Heart enough ...

to share and to care, to listen and to understand, and to make a loving home for my family.

Amen.

Acknowledgments

Thank you to Our Sunday Visitor for being so thoroughly professional and wonderfully kind to this novice author. I am especially grateful to Sarah Reinhard and Mary Beth Baker for holding my hand throughout the process, and to Claudia Volkman for her invaluable assistance in editing and polishing up the manuscript.

This book could not have come to fruition without the shared experiences and participation of the nearly six thousand members of the Catholic Working Mothers Facebook group. Their insights and feedback have been invaluable to the writing process. Ladies, thank you so much from the bottom of my heart.

Special thanks to Wendy Clark, who encouraged me to tackle this project when I wasn't sure I could do it. I also have everlasting gratitude for the current and former volunteer moderators of Catholic Working Mothers for helping me bring order to chaos (and keeping me sane in the bargain).

Last, but certainly not least, thanks be to God, from whom all blessings flow; Jesus, for being my rock; the Holy Spirit, for giving me wisdom and guidance; and Saint Gianna Beretta Molla, my patroness and my hero.

Notes

1. Wendy Wang, Kim Parker, and Paul Taylor, "Breadwinner Moms," Pew Research Center's Social & Demographic Trends Project, May 29, 2013, http://www.pewsocialtrends.org /2013/05/29/breadwinner-moms/.

2. Beulah Wood, *The People Paul Admired: The House Church Leaders of the New Testament* (Eugene, OR: Wipf and Stock, 2011), see cover image, https://wipfandstock.com /the-people-paul-admired.html (accessed September 30, 2018).

3. Catholic Online, "Saint Elizabeth Ann Seton," accessed September 30, 2018, https://www.catholic.org/saints /saint.php?saint_id=180.

4. Carmelite Sisters of Ireland, "Saint Louis & Saint Zélie Martin," accessed September 30, 2018, http://carmelitesisters.ie /saints-louis-zelie-martin/.

5. Society of the Little Flower, "The Early Years," accessed September 30, 2018, https://www.littleflower.org/therese /life-story/the-early-years/.

6. Edith Stein, *Essays on Woman (The Collected Works of Edith Stein, Vol. II)* Second Edition, ed. Dr. Lucy Gelber and Romaeus Leuven, O.C.D., trans. Freda Mary Oben, PhD (Washington, DC: ICS Publications, 1996), 79–80.

7. Vatican News Service, "Gianna Beretta Molla (1922– 1962)," The Holy See, accessed September 30, 2018, http://

www.vatican.va/news_services/liturgy/saints
/ns_lit_doc_20040516_beretta-molla_en.html.

8. Pietro Molla and Elio Guerriero, *Saint Gianna Molla:
Wife, Mother, Doctor,* trans. James G. Colbert (San Francisco:
Ignatius Press, 2004), 74.

9. United States Conference of Catholic Bishops, "Natural
Family Planning," accessed September 30, 2018, http://
www.usccb.org/issues-and-action/marriage-and-family
/natural-family-planning/index.cfm. To learn more about the
various methods of NFP, what the Church teaches about it, and
how it differs from birth control, check out the resources available on the USCCB website.

10. Brie Schwartz, "Anna Faris Keeps It Real About Life,
Love, and Everything In Between," *Redbook,* October 16, 2017,
https://www.redbookmag.com/life/news/a20277/anna-faris
-keeps-it-real-about-life-love-and-everything-in-between/.

11. Our Catholic Prayers, "Prayers for Offering Up Suffering," accessed September 30, 2018, https://
www.ourcatholicprayers.com/offering-prayers.html.

12. Josef Pieper, *The Four Cardinal Virtues* (Notre Dame,
IN: University of Notre Dame Press, 1966), 13–22.

13. Amanda Martinez Beck, "Potential vs. Capacity," *Em-
bracing This Good Body God Gave Me* (blog), November 8, 2016,
http://amandamartinezbeck.com/blog/2016/11/8
/my-fear-of-failure-potential-versus-capacity.

14. Pope Saint John Paul II, *Letter to Women,* The Holy See,
June 29, 1995, https://w2.vatican.va/content/john-paul-ii/en
/letters/1995/documents/hf_jp-ii_let_29061995_women.html,
sec. 2.

15. Molla and Guerriero, *Saint Gianna Molla,* 71.

16. Stein, *Essays on Woman,* 80.

17. Sherrie Bourg Carter, PsyD, "Why Mess Causes Stress:
8 Reasons, 8 Remedies," *Psychology Today,* March 14, 2012,

https://www.psychologytoday.com/us/blog/high-octane
-women/201203/why-mess-causes-stress-8-reasons-8
-remedies.

18. CatholicMom, "Finding God in the Housework," July 4,
2011, http://catholicmom.com/2011/07/04/finding-god
-in-the-housework/.

19. U.S. Equal Employment Opportunity Commission,
"Pregnancy Discrimination," accessed September 30, 2018,
https://www.eeoc.gov/eeoc/publications/fs-preg.cfm.

20. U.S. Equal Employment Opportunity Commission,
"Harassment," accessed September 30, 2018, https://
www.eeoc.gov/laws/types/harassment.cfm

21. Drew DeSilver, "Access to Paid Family Leave Varies
Widely Across Employers, Industries," Pew Research Center,
March 23, 2017, http://www.pewresearch.org
/fact-tank/2017/03/23/access-to-paid-family-leave-varies
-widely-across-employers-industries/.

22. Rebecca Greenfield, "More Companies Than Ever Offer
Paid Parental Leave," Bloomberg, June 28, 2018,
https://www.bloomberg.com/news/articles/2018-06-28
/more-companies-than-ever-offer-paid-parental-leave.

23. Wage and Hour Division, United States Department
of Labor, "Fact Sheet #28: The Family and Medical Leave Act,"
accessed September 30, 2018, https://www.dol.gov/whd/regs
/compliance/whdfs28.pdf.

24. United States Breastfeeding Committee, "Your Rights
As a Breastfeeding Employee," KellyMom.com, February 8,
2018, https://kellymom.com/bf/pumpingmoms
/employed-moms/your-rights-as-a-breastfeeding-employee/.

25. Jon M. Taylor, MBA, PhD, "The Case (for and) against
Multi-level Marketing," Federal Trade Commission, 2011,
https://www.ftc.gov/sites/default/files/documents/public
_comments/trade-regulation-rule-disclosure

-requirements-and-prohibitions-concerning-business
-opportunities-ftc.r511993-00017%C2%A0/00017-57317.pdf.

26. Check out the excellent podcast "The Dream" for an in-depth investigation about MLMs and their history: https://www.stitcher.com/podcast/stitcher/the-dream.

27. United States Conference of Catholic Bishops, "When I Call for Help: A Pastoral Response to Domestic Violence Against Women," accessed September 30, 2018, http://www.usccb.org/issues-and-action/marriage-and-family/marriage/domestic-violence/when-i-call-for-help.cfm.

28. Gregory K. Popcak, *For Better … Forever: A Catholic Guide to Lifelong Marriage* (Huntington, IN: Our Sunday Visitor, 2015).

29. United States Conference of Catholic Bishops, "Annulment," accessed September 30, 2018, http://www.usccb.org/issues-and-action/marriage-and-family/marriage/annulment/index.cfm.

30. Simcha Fisher, *The Sinner's Guide to Natural Family Planning* (Huntington, IN: Our Sunday Visitor, 2014), 73–77.

31. U.S. Equal Employment Opportunity Commission, "The ADA: Your Responsibilities as an Employer," accessed September 30, 2018, https://www.eeoc.gov/eeoc/publications/ada17.cfm.

32. NAMI: National Alliance on Mental Illness, "Mental Health by the Numbers," accessed September 30, 2018, https://www.nami.org/Learn-More/Mental-Health-By-the-Numbers.

33. Jennifer Peepas, "#450: How to Tighten up Your Game at Work When You're Depressed," Captain Awkward, February 16, 2013, https://captainawkward.com/2013/02/16/450-how-to-tighten-up-your-game-at-work-when-youre-depressed/.

34. Pope Saint John Paul II, "Homily of John Paul II: Apostolic Pilgrimage to Bangladesh, Singapore, Fiji Islands, New Zealand, Australia, and Seychelles," November 30, 1986, https://

w2.vatican.va/content/john-paul-ii/en/homilies/1986
/documents/hf_jp-ii_hom_19861130_perth-australia.html,
sec. 4.

35. Rebecca Frech, *Can We Be Friends?* (Huntington, IN:
Our Sunday Visitor, 2018), 9–10.

36. Christy Isinger and Haley Stewart, "FoC 086: Living
Out Your Creative Dreams to Love Your Family with Jennifer
Fulwiler," Fountains of Carrots, May 1, 2018, http://
fountainsofcarrots.com/foc-086/

37. Olga Phoenix, "Self-Care Wheel," Olga Phoenix Project:
Healing for Social Change, http://www.olgaphoenix.com
/wp-content/uploads/2015/05/Self-Care-Wheel-template
-English.pdf.

38. Beliefnet, "Working Mother's Prayer," accessed September 30, 2018, http://www.beliefnet.com/prayers/catholic
/parenting/working-mothers-prayer.aspx.

39. Catholic Online, "Prayer to Saint Joseph for Success in
Work," accessed September 30, 2018, https://www.catholic.org
/prayers/prayer.php?p=780.

40. Families.com, "Refresh Your Spirit: Prayers for Single
Parents," accessed September 30, 2018, https://
www.families.com/refresh-your-spirit-prayers-for-single-p.

About the Author

JoAnna Wahlund was baptized, raised, and married in the Evangelical Lutheran Church in America. In May 2003, two weeks after graduating from the University of Minnesota Twin Cities with a degree in English, she converted to Catholicism. A North Dakota native, she fled the frigid frozen north for the sunny skies of Arizona in 2008. She has six terrific kids here on earth, four saints in heaven praying for her, and a wonderful husband of seventeen years who supports her in all things. She worked outside the home as an editor for more than a decade, but now works as chief cook and bottle washer for La Casa Wahlund in addition to her volunteer role as senior editor for CatholicStand.com. Her website is www.catholicworkingmom.com.